POINT COUNTERPOINT

Discussion and Persuasion Techniques

George W. Pifer

Nancy Whisler Mutoh

NEWBURY HOUSE PUBLISHERS
A division of Harper & Row, Publishers, Inc.
Cambridge, New York, Philadelphia, San Francisco, Washington, D.C.
London, Mexico City, São Paulo, Singapore, Sidney

Director: Laurie E. Likoff
Production Coordinator: Cynthia Funkhouser
Text and Cover Design: Suzanne Bennett Associates
Text Art: Loring Eutemey
Compositor: Crane Typesetting Service, Inc.
Printer and Binder: Malloy Lithographing, Inc.

NEWBURY HOUSE PUBLISHERS
A Division of Harper & Row, Publishers, Inc.
Language Science
Language Teaching
Language Learning

Point Counterpoint: Discussion and Persuasion Techniques

Library of Congress Cataloging in Publication Data
Pifer, George W.
    Point counterpoint : discussion and persuasion techniques / George
W. Pifer, Nancy Whisler Mutoh.
        p.   cm.
    ISBN 0-06-632403-3
    1. English language—Textbooks for foreign speakers.
2. Discussion. 3. Persuasion (Rhetoric) I. Mutoh, Nancy Whisler.
II. Title.
PE1128.P487   1988
428.3'4—dc19   88-6914
                                                                   CIP

63-24032   First printing: April 1988
Printed in the U.S.A.   88 89 90 91 9 8 7 6 5 4 3 2 1

Contents

Introduction

Point Counterpoint is intended for intermediate- and advanced-level students of English as a Second or Foreign Language who are working on developing successful discussion skills. The techniques presented are intended to give students the language necessary to resolve personal dilemmas, to consider both sides of a controversial subject, and to be persuasive in discussions of broad social significance about which they have strong personal convictions.

The following assumptions guided the development of this material, which we find in actual classroom use to be practical, flexible, and successful.

Students Need to Succeed

Many people hesitate to speak up in groups, especially in a foreign language, for cultural and/or personal reasons. Lack of confidence is one of the most common reasons. Students need to accumulate "successful experiences" in discussion in order to have the confidence and desire to use and improve their English. Good discussion material must be structured so that almost any group of students will have good discussions without long silences and meaningless wandering.

From Passive to Active Knowledge

Most students know more English than they actually use, as do native speakers. Unfortunately, nonnative speakers often resign themselves to simple-sounding, sometimes even childish, statements. But with appropriate material, they can be guided to discuss at a level closer to their own maturity and intelligence. Good material should first teach (or reteach) high-frequency communicative devices, such as questioning, qualifying, agreeing/disagreeing, emphasizing, substantiating, generalizing, and clarifying. Secondly, it should offer a structured approach to discussion with activities that cause the students to use those communicative devices when discussing an interesting subject.

Effective by English Standards

We recognize that students can use rhetorical devices and logic systems to express ideas in ways considered more or less effective in their own languages. But their systems of rhetoric and logic may resemble English closely or hardly at all. We assume, however, that students studying English want to use it effectively and persuasively, as judged by English speakers.

Organization of the Text

Part 1: Dilemmas of Daily Life

Exercises: Before Class
1. Read and Decide
2. Review

In Class
3. Retell (summarize main points in reading)
4. Rethink (pairs discuss how variations in elements of the reading affect their decisions)
5. Generalize (small groups discuss similar kinds of situations)
6. Role Play (students prepare for and present role play)

Units 4, 8, and 11 have ranking exercises instead of readings, as a change of pace.

Part 2: Toward Argumentation

Exercises: Before Class
1. Read and Consider (two points of view are presented)
2. Review

In Class
3. Retell
4. Analyze the Content (pairs discuss questions about the points made in each argument)
5. Analyze the Structure (teacher leads class discussion)
6. Generalize (small groups discuss questions raised by the nature of the topic)
7. Role Play (students prepare for and present role play)

Part 3: Argumentation

Exercises: Before Class
1. Read and Evaluate (strong points of view are presented; "for" and "against")

In Class
2. Retell
3. Analyze the Content (pairs check phrases representing main points in each argument, identifying the sentences in the dialog)

4. Analysis of Discussion Techniques (teacher leads class discussion)
5. Practice (pairs work with discussion techniques, identifying them in the dialog)
6. Discuss (small groups have general discussion based on or related to the topic, making an effort to use the discussion techniques)
7. Role Play (students prepare for and present a role play, encouraged to be very persuasive)

The introductions to each part describe the content and goals of the section. It is useful to work through these with your students, and encouraging to them to summarize how much they have learned in the course of the lessons. Understanding objectives and meeting them keeps students motivated.

Notice that, especially early in the text, the Retell exercise asks students to make notes on the board as other students give responses in summarizing the elements of the reading. This develops quick "on-your-feet" thinking and the ability to pick out a few words from a longer response. It will prove useful in helping students make the transfer to note-taking skills in other courses. These notes can be referred to as students work in pairs discussing variations of the dilemmas in Part 1.

In Parts 1 and 2, students are encouraged to write a few notes to help them prepare for the role play. It will get them started. You may wish to allow them to use their notes as they perform the role play, especially at first.

In Part 3, there is less of this kind of aid. Students will be more comfortable with the flow of the lesson, and their success breeds success.

The teacher is encouraged to let the students do the talking in the exercises, except for the Analysis of Discussion Techniques. They will need your guidance here, and your ability to give other examples, beyond those given in the text for each of the techniques, in order to reach complete understanding. Keep the exercise as brief as possible, however, so that your students can begin using the new language right away. As always, the more talking they do, the better. It is through countless repetitions of language forms in meaningful discussion that fluency develops.

PART 1

DILEMMAS OF DAILY LIFE

Introduction

Sometimes it is easy to make decisions. You may find yourself in one of the following situations:

- [ ] You are standing in line and someone steps in front of you. You can tell her the line forms at the rear.
- [ ] A friend is drunk, but he wants to drive. You can tell him that you must take his keys and drive him home.
- [ ] You see someone stealing office supplies where you work. You can report her to the boss.

In these cases, making a decision is easy. But what do you do when:

- [ ] The person who steps in front of you in the line is a large, very strong man, and he is angry?
- [ ] The drunk person who wants to drive is your boss?
- [ ] The person stealing office supplies is your friend, and she says she doesn't take much, and "everybody does it"?

These situations are called dilemmas because there is no easy way to decide what to do. Discussing possible solutions to dilemmas is a good first step toward developing argumentative skills, because each dilemma is examined in depth and from many angles.

> Skills you will develop in Part 1 include:
> Qualifying and clarifying opinions
> Generalizing a principle from several situations
> Understanding and reflecting on other people's feelings

You'll acquire these skills first by reading about the situation before class, then by deciding what you would do in that situation and reviewing the material. In class, you or one of your classmates will retell the situation. You will rethink what you would do by changing elements of the situation. You will generalize the principles involved and transfer them to other situations. Finally, you will role-play a dilemma.

1. Waiting in Line

Have strangers ever bothered you in public—for example, by stepping in front of you in a line, or by blowing smoke in your face in a crowded room? How did you handle the situation? Did you know what to say?

Before class

1. Read and Decide

Read the story, imagining that you are in this situation, and decide what you would do.

progress

You have just finished a long day at work and are waiting at the bus stop to catch a bus home. At this time of day, the buses are nearly full by the time they reach your stop. Each bus that stops has space for only a few passengers. Little by little, however, you **work your way** to the head of the line. After waiting almost half an hour, you are fifth from the head of the line. You hope to get on the next bus.

enter (the line) out of turn

At this point, a group of four people **cuts in** ahead of you. You are afraid they might ruin your chances of getting on the next bus. What do you do?

2. Review

Practice answering the questions without looking at the text.

1. Where are you going?
2. At this time of day, why do you usually have to wait for several buses to come before you can finally board one?
3. After waiting half an hour, what is your position in line?
4. What happens then?

In class

3. Retell

Members of the class may volunteer to tell about the events as they happened in the situation. Your teacher or a student may want to list the events on the chalkboard as a quick review.

Here are some cues:

1. What's the time of day?
2. Where are you waiting? For what?
3. Why are you waiting? What's the problem?
4. After waiting half an hour, where in the line are you?
5. What happens then?
6. Why does it bother you?

4. Rethink

Work with a partner. Explain what you would do in this situation. Then discuss how the variations listed below might affect your decision.

1. The weather is fine./It's cold and raining.
2. It's daytime./It's late evening.
3. It's rush hour and the buses are nearly full./It's the middle of the day and the buses are half-empty.
4. You are near the head of the line./You are far back in the line.
5. Four students cut in line./A little old lady cuts in./A drunk cuts in.
6. You are tired and anxious to get home./You are in no great hurry.

5. Generalize

Work in small groups. Discuss with the members of your group how you would handle the following situations. Consider that we all sometimes feel uncomfortable or annoyed by the actions of strangers, but we may hesitate to complain. Have you ever been in a situation like this? Tell about it.

1. You are in a public place, such as a bus, elevator, or movie theater, where smoking is prohibited, and someone is smoking. Do you say anything? If so, what?

2. You and a friend go out for dinner. You are disappointed when the waiter brings you a dinner you didn't order. If you send the food back, you will have to wait while your friend is eating and the correct meal is being prepared. If you keep it, you will have to be satisfied with something you don't particularly care for. What do you do?

3. You are on a crowded train platform with your young child. The person standing next to you is holding a lighted cigarette and does not seem to notice that the cigarette is very close to your child's face. You think that it's dangerous to smoke in such a crowded place, even though smoking is not prohibited. Do you say anything? If so, what?

4. You are riding on a bus. You think the driver is unnecessarily rough and careless. He brakes and accelerates suddenly, causing danger and discomfort to the people who are standing. Do you say anything? If so, what?

6. Role Play

A. Getting Ready

Sometimes it is best to complain in a polite, pleasant way. Sometimes we need to be more forceful. For each of the situations in the **Generalize** section, write down several ways that you could complain. What could you say to the person smoking in a movie theater?

Examples: Get rid of that cigarette!
The sign says "No Smoking."
There's no smoking here. Would you mind putting out your cigarette?

_____

_____

_____

_____

B. Act It Out

Role-play Situation 4, about the careless bus driver. One person will be the complaining passenger, and another will be the bus driver, who is tired of the heavy traffic and is late meeting his schedule. The passenger will begin by complaining politely and pleasantly, but will gradually become more forceful.

2. A Good Future

How much influence should a parent have over a teenager's future?

Before class

1. Read and Decide

Read the story and decide what you would do in this situation.

wife or husband

savings plan for old age

You and your **spouse** own a grocery store. You are proud of your business, which took many years to build, though you have to work very long hours and get no vacations. You have no **pension** plan, and you hope that your health lasts long enough for you to educate your children and save some money for your old age.

When you were young, you didn't have the chance to continue your schooling. But things are different now, and you have bigger plans for your daughter. You want her to get a good government or company job, with the **security** of pension and medical benefits, vacations and shorter working hours.

safety

Your daughter, however, hates school and loves to join you at the store every afternoon after school, instead of doing her homework. She insists that she doesn't want to continue in school next year. She says she wants to learn the grocery business from you and eventually **take over** the store. She's a smart girl, and you think her bad grades are just a result of not studying.

manage

believes in

You have had many arguments on this subject. Your daughter is **convinced of** her own desires. You are equally convinced that you know what's really best for her in the long run. If you were the parent, what would you do? If you were the daughter, what would you do?

2. Review

Practice answering the questions without looking at the text.

1. Why don't you want your daughter to follow you in the grocery business?
2. What hopes do you have for your daughter's future?
3. How does your daughter feel about school? About the grocery store? About her future?

In class

3. Retell

Your teacher may ask two or three students to tell about the events as they happened in the situation. Another student may want to list the events on the chalkboard as a quick review. Here are some cues:

1. Is the business that you started with your spouse doing well?
2. Do you have savings for your old age?
3. What do you want your daughter to do?
4. What does she want to do?
5. Have you and your daughter made a final decision about her future?

4. Rethink

Work with a partner. Explain what you would do in the situation. Then discuss how the variations listed below might affect your decision.

1. It's your son, not your daughter, who wants to quit school and work with you.
2. Your child doesn't want to work in the family business, or for the government or a company. He or she wants to study art.
3. Your child has reached the legal, minimum age for quitting school./ He or she has finished high school and doesn't want to go to college.
4. Your son or daughter appears to have the ability to do well in school./He or she could probably never be a good student, even with a lot of studying.

5. Generalize

Work in small groups. Discuss with the members of your group how you would handle the following situations. Consider that all parents sometimes feel, judging from their own experiences, that they know what is best for their children. The children, however, don't always agree.

1. You want your daughter to finish school and then marry some nice man. But she wants to go into business.
2. You have built a successful business, hoping that one of your children would take it over from you. Unfortunately, none of them appears very interested and you don't know how much to insist.
3. You know that friends can have a great influence—for good or for bad—on a child. That's why you are worried. Your child's friends are not very interested in school, and they tend to be wild and not well-behaved. Your child is good, but you are certain that these friends will be a bad influence. You don't know how much you can or should interfere in your child's choice of friends.

6. Role Play

A. Getting Ready

Any young person would have some strong feelings about his or her future. Write down some points that you would want to make if you were discussing the matter with your parents.

Examples: I'm old enough to make my own decisions.
I know what's best for me.

_____

_____

_____

_____

B. Act It Out

Choose one of the situations from your group discussion and act out the conversation. Two people will be the parents and another person will be the son or daughter.

3. Mealtime Tug-of-War

A parent's concept of acceptable table manners usually differs greatly from a young child's. How can a parent train a stubborn child without resorting to constant nagging and criticizing?

Before class

1. Read and Decide

Read the story carefully, and decide what you would do in this situation.

fussy, difficult-to-please

Your five-year-old daughter is a very slow, **picky** eater. At mealtime, she can waste up to an hour playing with her food, talking, and daydreaming instead of eating. This is especially annoying in the morning, when everyone has to leave for school and work.

You think it is important for her to eat a good breakfast, but your efforts to speed up her eating have failed. You don't want to make a big issue out of such a minor thing because you are afraid it might get worse instead of better. At the same time, though, you are tired of this tug-of-war every morning. What do you think could be the cause(s) of your daughter's eating habits? What should you do?

2. Review

Practice answering the questions without looking at the text.

1. Describe the way that your daughter eats.
2. Why is this a problem in the morning?
3. You could solve the problem by simply letting her skip breakfast. Why don't you?
4. What is your dilemma?

In class

3. Retell

Your teacher may ask two or three students to tell about the problem described in the situation. Another student may want to list the points on the chalkboard as a quick review. Here are some cues:

1. How does your daughter behave at the breakfast table?
2. Why does it matter?
3. What are your choices in dealing with the problem?

4. Rethink

Work with a partner. Explain what you would do in this situation. Then discuss how the variations listed below might affect your decision.

1. Your child is two/five/eight/twelve years old.
2. The child is a son/a daughter.
3. Your child attends afternoon kindergarten, so there is no worry about her being late for school.
4. She is a slow eater because you want her to eat a "good breakfast," although she doesn't seem to be very hungry in the morning.
5. She's willing to eat, but wants cookies instead of the healthful food the rest of the family eats.

5. Generalize

Work in small groups. Discuss with the members of your group how you would handle the following situations. Consider that parents want their children to learn acceptable social behavior and cooperation. At the same time, however, they don't want to be constantly criticizing and scolding them. The problem is how to be strict enough but not too strict. Discuss how each person in your group would handle these situations. Have you or your friends experienced these or similar problems? Tell about them and how they were handled.

1. Your child has terrible table manners that annoy you at home and embarrass you in front of friends. What table manners do you think are important for a young child to learn?
2. Your child has started throwing temper tantrums. The other day, you were in a store and your child kept asking you to buy toys and candy. When you said no, he/she started pounding the floor with his fists and crying violently.
3. Your two children fight frequently and sometimes violently. What do you think are the acceptable limits of children's fighting?

6. Role Play

A. Getting Ready

Parents may differ strongly in their views about controlling their child's behavior. How can they express their strong views to each other without losing their tempers? Write down some arguments to

be made in favor of strictness or gentleness in dealing with a child.
Here are some cues:

Spare the rod and spoil the child.
That child is embarrassing our whole family.
Do you want your child to fear you?
Kindness and reason are the ways to get a willing response.

_____

_____

_____

_____

B. Act It Out

Choose one of the situations from your group discussion and act out
the conversation between the parents. One parent favors being strict
and one doesn't.

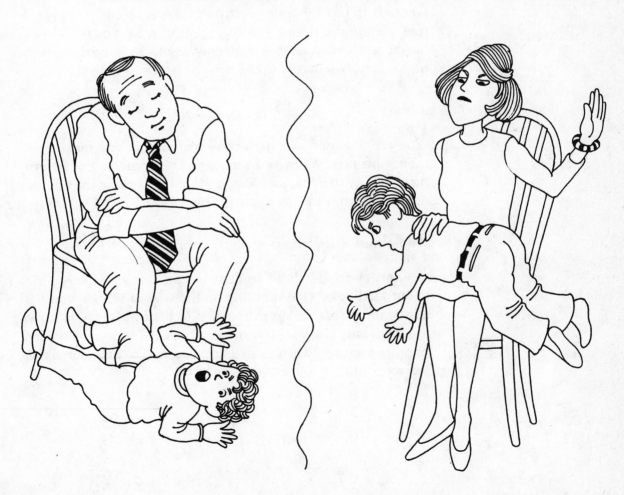

4. Little White Lies

Do you ever "stretch" the truth? Do you think it is acceptable to exaggerate, deny, or keep quiet about the truth under certain circumstances?

Before class

1. Read and Decide

Read each situation below. Put a number "1" in front of the "lies" that you think are definitely wrong, a "2" in front of those that you feel are borderline (neither clearly right nor clearly wrong), and a "3" in front of those that you think are all right.

A Teenaged Student

_____ You are a student in need of a summer job. Your parents expect you to help pay for your education. One problem, however, is that the minimum legal working age is sixteen. You're thirteen, but bigger than the average thirteen-year-old, so when the woman hiring factory workers asks your age, you say sixteen.

A Waiter

_____ You are a waiter in a high-class restaurant. You make good money on tips. When you report your income to the government for income tax purposes, you underestimate the amount of income from tips by about 20 percent.

A Grade-School Student

being late

_____ You are a grade-school student whose teacher is very strict about **tardiness**. One morning on the way to school, you find a little puppy on the street and stop to play with it. You arrive at school late, and your teacher is angry. You say you were late because your mother was sick and you had to make breakfast for yourself and your little sister.

16

A Friend of New Parents

_____ Your friends just had a baby. You go to their house to congratulate them and take a gift. When you look at the baby, you think it is simply ugly. You look at the parents' expectant faces, however, and say, "What a cute baby!"

A Worker in a Store

goods, the things the store sells

stealing

_____ You work in a sporting goods store. You know that the other clerk is stealing **merchandise** because you saw him do it. The manager tells you one day that there has been an increase in **shoplifting**. He asks you if you've seen anything, and you say no.

Selling Your Car

condition

_____ You are selling your used car. It's six years old, but the engine is in pretty good **shape** and the body isn't too rusty. The problem is that the clutch is beginning to wear out. Because that's an expensive repair, you decided to sell the car. When people come to look at the car, you point out all its good points and tell them the car is in excellent condition, considering its age.

In class

2. Retell

Members of the class may volunteer to describe each situation. One student may write the title of each situation on the chalkboard, and just a phrase or two to remind everyone about it. Another student may ask the class to raise their hands if they ranked the situation as 1, 2, or 3. Write the tally (total number) on the chalkboard next to each title.

Example: <u>1</u> <u>2</u> <u>3</u>
        7 3 5

Remember: 1 = wrong, 2 = borderline, 3 = all right.

3. Rethink

Work with a partner. Compare your evaluations of the situations. Discuss the circumstances behind each lie and alternative ways of handling each situation.

4. Generalize

Work in small groups. Discuss with the members of your group how you would respond to the following:

1. A "little white lie" is a lie that people don't consider serious or wrong. Which of the above would you consider little white lies? Why do people tell little white lies?
2. Give some examples from daily life when people use little white lies to get out of awkward situations.

5. Role Play

A. Getting Ready

Work with a partner. Figure out a situation requiring a little white lie. Decide which of you will play each role. Make it humorous. Have fun with this.

B. Act It Out

Each pair of students may quickly perform their situation for the class.

5. Me a Thief?

Do you think that stealing is ever right? What if it's accidental?

Before class

1. Read and Decide

Read the story and decide what you would do in this situation.

You go into a self-service store that sells all kinds of household goods, home repair tools, and children's toys. You pick up a shopping basket at the door. You walk up and down the aisles, choosing the items you want and putting them in the basket. When you have collected the things you need, you go to the check-out line, pay for your purchases, and leave.

When you get home, however, you realize that you mistakenly put a small screwdriver that you wanted in your shirt pocket instead of in the shopping basket. You went through the check-out line without paying for it. You could go back to the store, explain what happened, and pay for the screwdriver. Or you could consider it a lucky accident, avoid the **nuisance** of going back, and just keep your "free" screwdriver. After all, the store wouldn't lose much on such a small item. What do you do?

bother

2. Review

Practice answering the questions without looking at the text.

1. What kinds of things does the store sell?
2. What does the customer have to do in a self-service store?
3. When you get home, what do you realize?
4. What two choices do you have now?

In class

3. Retell

Your teacher may ask a student to think of a question to ask about the situation. Members of the class may volunteer to answer the question. Someone may write notes (short paraphrases) from the answers on the chalkboard.

4. Rethink

Work with a partner. Explain what you would do in the situation. Then discuss how the variations listed below might affect your decision.

1. The item you picked up is quite inexpensive./It is quite expensive.
2. The store is a large chain store./It is a small, family-owned business.
3. You are alone when you discover your mistake./You are with family or friends.
4. The store is close to your home./It is quite far away.
5. You have plenty of money to pay for the item./You don't have much money.
6. You think that the merchandise at the store is overpriced./You think that the prices are very reasonable.

5. Generalize

Work in small groups. Discuss with the members of your group how you would respond in the following circumstances. Have you ever been in a similar situation? Tell about it and how you handled it.

1. You are in a restaurant and the waitress forgets to include the dessert on the bill.
2. You are buying stamps in the post office. The clerk, thinking you had paid with a larger bill, gives you too much change.
3. You borrowed a book from a friend. You have had it so long that you are embarrassed to return it, and now you can't even find it. Perhaps your friend has forgotten about the book, too.

6. Role Play

A. Getting Ready

Using a situation from your group discussion, or another one, prepare a monologue, in the form of an argument with yourself, about what you are going to do about the situation. Write some notes to remind yourself of the points to make in the argument you will have with yourself.

_____

_____

_____

_____

B. Act It Out

Your teacher may ask each member of the class to tell the subject of his/her situation. The teacher or the class may ask a few students to do their role plays for everyone.

6. Speaking Up

What do you do if a person who generally acts in your best interests (for example, a friend or relative) seems to be acting against them? Do you find it hard to express your anxiety?

1. Read and Decide

Read the story and decide what you would do in this situation.

come for you, meet you

understand your indirect comment

It's pouring rain. You're glad that your friend offered you a ride, so you don't have to get wet waiting for the bus. It was also nice of your friend to go out of her way to **pick you up** at your house.

There are puddles on the road in places, and it looks slippery. Your friend is driving just a little over the speed limit, but in your opinion too fast for the road and the weather conditions. You say something about having plenty of time, but your friend doesn't **get the hint**. You're beginning to worry about your safety, and you wish she would slow down. Do you say something, and, if so, what? Or do you trust your friend's judgment and driving skill and keep quiet?

2. Review

Practice answering the questions without looking at the text.

1. Describe the weather and the road conditions.
2. Why do you feel grateful to your friend?
3. Why are you worried about the way that your friend is driving?
4. What two choices do you have now?

3. Retell

Members of the class may volunteer to describe all the details of:

1. The circumstances
2. The problem

Another student may list the details on the chalkboard under the two headings.

4. Rethink

Work with a partner. Explain what you would do in the situation. Then discuss how the variations listed below might affect your decision.

1. You and your friend are alone in the car./Your family is also in the car.
2. The weather is good, the road is dry, and you don't think there is much danger, although your friend is going over the posted speed limit.
3. Your friend is a very skilled driver./He or she is a new driver without much experience.
4. When your friend comes to your house to pick you up, you think he/she may have been drinking.
5. The driver is your friend/a relative/your boss.
6. The driver is younger than you/older/about the same age.

5. Generalize

Work in small groups. Discuss with the members of your group how you would respond in the following circumstances. Consider that friends sometimes do things that frighten, annoy, or anger us, and yet we may hesitate to complain. Have you experienced any problems of this type? Tell about them.

1. You are a teenager. Your parents don't want you to drink (or take drugs) and you yourself have no great desire to, either. You are at a party with friends where there is liquor (drugs). Your friends laugh when you say, "No thanks," and they keep trying to make you change your mind.
2. You are meeting a friend of yours to go see a movie. This friend is almost never on time. Even though you have complained to him/her in a joking way, you still usually find yourself waiting. You have now been waiting about fifteen minutes and you think the movie will start very soon.

6. Role Play

A. Getting Ready

Think about ways you could tell your friend that he/she is driving too fast. Your teacher may want to list them on the chalkboard and give you ideas for more ways to express yourself.

B. Act It Out

1. Several people may act out the situation about drinking or taking drugs in number 1, above.
2. Two people may act out the conversation in number 2, after the friend finally arrives twenty minutes late.

7. To Tell the Truth

Would you tell someone an important truth (that concerns him or her) if the knowledge might have a destructive effect on the person?

Before class

1. Read and Decide

Read the story, imagining that you are the doctor. Decide what you would do.

He came to you, complaining of stomach pains that he had been having for about six months. You tell him that he shouldn't have waited so long before investigating the cause. He replies that he didn't think it was anything serious, probably just nerves, because he's been worrying about some family problems.

detailed, thorough
surgery to find out a
patient's internal
condition

You conduct **extensive** tests and recommend **exploratory surgery**, because you suspect cancer. When you tell him your suspicion, he agrees to the surgery. During the operation, you discover that he has extensive cancer that has already spread to other organs. His situation seems hopeless to you, and you think it is only a question of how much time he has left.

chemical treatment

You will have to tell him that he has cancer, because you want to recommend **chemotherapy**. You don't know, however, whether you should tell him the whole truth. On the one hand, you think he has enough to worry about with his family problems. Perhaps knowing the truth about his own health might be more than he could stand. You don't want to ruin what time he has left. On the other hand, you feel that he may want to know the truth so that he can deal with his family difficulties in a realistic way and make arrangements for his **dependents**. What do you do?

wife if she is not
holding a paying job,
and children

2. Review

Practice answering the questions without looking at the text.

1. Why did the man come to see you?
2. How long has he had this problem?
3. Why didn't he come to you sooner?
4. How do you investigate his problem?
5. What do you discover during the operation?
6. What treatment do you want to recommend?
7. Why do you think that it might be best not to tell him the whole truth? Why do you think that perhaps you should tell him everything?

In class

3. Retell

One student may describe the patient's physical condition. Another may explain the doctor's dilemma. Two other students can write notes on the chalkboard under each heading. One will write notes under "Physical Condition" and the other under "Dilemma."

4. Rethink

Work with a partner. Explain what you would do in the situation if you were the doctor. Then discuss how the variations listed below might affect your decision.

1. The patient is a man/a woman.
2. When the patient mentioned family problems, he/she was referring to money difficulties/marital problems/another sick family member.
3. The patient is married with children./The patient is single.
4. The patient is a child/middle-aged/elderly.
5. The patient is religious/has no religion.
6. The patient appears to you to have a strong, mature character./ The patient appears to have a weak, excitable character.

5. Generalize

Work in small groups. Consider that sometimes we have to decide whether to tell someone the truth even if that knowledge might cause problems. How would each member of your group handle these situations?

1. You wonder whether you should tell your adopted child about his/her real parents, and, if so, when and how.
2. Your child needs major surgery and asks you what's going to happen at the hospital and whether it will hurt. You wonder how much to explain.
3. You have a good friend whose spouse is having an affair (has another lover). Should you tell your friend?

6. Role Play

A. Getting Ready

Think about the situation in number 2, above. Write down some ideas to prepare yourself to be the parent who must have this conversation with your child.

_____

_____

_____

_____

B. Act It Out

One student plays the role of the parent and another the child. The child, of course, is a little frightened. If another student would handle the parent's role differently, there can be a second role play.

8. They Owe It to Me

Could you justify cheating or stealing from big organizations, such as companies, government organizations, or hotels, on the grounds that (a) they'll never miss what you're taking, (b) they've already overcharged you for it, or (c) you deserve it for some other reason?

Before class

1. Read and Decide

Read each situation below. Put a "1" in front of the actions that you think are definitely wrong, a "2" in front of those that you feel are borderline (neither clearly right nor clearly wrong), and a "3" in front of those that you think are all right.

Avoiding the Cost of a Telephone Call

_____ When you arrive at your destination, you make a long-distance call to your home, person-to-person to yourself. Before leaving, you told your family that this phone call would be your signal to them that you had arrived safely. Of course, they'll tell the operator you are not at home. (Note: with person-to-person calls, there is no charge if the person requested is not there.)

Getting Overtime Pay

_____ Your work is paid by the hour. During regular working hours, you sometimes work slowly, leaving some of the work for overtime, which pays you 50 percent more.

Taking Company Supplies

_____ You sometimes take home company pens and pencils, which your family uses.

Not Acknowledging a Computer Error

_____ You subscribe to a magazine, but because of a computer error the company sends you two copies of the same magazine each week. You don't tell them about the mistake and give the extra magazines to a friend.

Taking Objects from Hotels

_____ Whenever you stay in hotels, you take all the stationery, envelopes, and post cards provided for guests. You sometimes also take an ashtray or a towel.

A Full Day's Work

_____ You are a civil servant whose office hours are 8:30 AM to 5:00 PM. Like most of your fellow workers, you arrive in the morning a half-hour late and leave a half-hour early. On payday, however, you accept a paycheck for a full work week.

Padding Your Expense Account

exaggerating money provided by the company for business trips and entertaining

_____ In order to avoid taxes, your company lets employees know that some **padding** of **expense accounts** would not be investigated or punished. So you include items on your expense account that are not actual business expenses, and keep the extra money for yourself.

In class

2. Retell

Members of the class may volunteer to describe each situation. One student may write the title of each situation on the chalkboard, and just a phrase or two to remind everyone about it. Another student may ask members of the class to raise their hands if they ranked the situation as 1, 2, or 3. Write the tally (total number) on the chalkboard next to each title.

      Example: <u>1</u> <u>2</u> <u>3</u>
                     2 8 5

Remember: 1 = wrong, 2 = borderline, 3 = all right.

3. Rethink

Work with a partner. Compare your ranking of each cheating situation. Explain your answers, especially your feelings about those you marked as borderline.

4. Generalize

Work in small groups. Discuss with the members of your group the following ways people think about and behave about cheating the government or a business.

deserve it, have earned it

1. Some people feel that the government and big business take a lot of money from them. They feel it's all right to get some of it back. They say, "They owe it to me" or "I've **got it coming**." Discuss the reasons people give for behaving in the ways described above.
2. There are many ways, big and small, of cheating the government or big business. What other ways have you heard of?

5. Role Play

A. Getting Ready

Members of each group will work out a role play for number 2, above, choosing *one* of the other ways people cheat the government or big business. Write down some notes to use in describing it. Then share your notes with the other members of your group. Decide which ideas to use. Select one person from your group to role-play the person who does the cheating.

B. Act It Out

The person doing the role play must try to be convincing about the
"fairness" or "appropriateness" of her/his actions.

9. Marriage on the Rocks

"On the rocks" has two meanings in this story. Like a ship on a rocky seacoast, a marriage on the rocks is in trouble and unlikely to survive. "On the rocks" is also an expression that describes a way of serving alcohol, such as whiskey, that heavy drinkers often prefer. The whiskey is poured over ice cubes ("rocks") undiluted (no water or mix is added). Why are both meanings of "on the rocks" appropriate in the following situation?

Before class

1. Read and Decide

Read the story carefully, and decide what you would do in this dilemma.

Your spouse has a drinking problem. When you realized that it was serious and could destroy your family, you discussed it frankly. He/she admitted it and promised to stop drinking. That was several years ago. Since then, the same promise has been made and broken many times.

You are beginning to lose hope. The family finances are suffering. You are also worried that seeing their parent drunk so often is having a bad effect on your children. As time passes, you are afraid that the drinking problem will get worse. As the children grow older, you are afraid they will come to hate their mother/father and feel ashamed. You are also tired of trying to keep the drinking a secret and pretending to your friends that everything is fine.

The last time that your spouse tried to stop drinking, you felt optimistic. You went together to a meeting of Alcoholics Anonymous, an organization that has helped many alcoholics to stop drinking. Because your hopes were so high, you became terribly disappointed when that effort failed and the drinking started again. You told your parents about the problem and they suggested a divorce. They said the drinking and arguing would hurt the children more than a divorce would. They also felt that the shock of asking for the divorce might help your spouse stop **permanently** drinking **once and for all**. You don't like any of the options available, but you have to do something. What do you do?

2. Review

Practice answering the questions without looking at the text.

1. When did you first decide to discuss the drinking problem frankly?
2. What happened as a result of that discussion?
3. What present and future bad effects of the drinking problem are you worried about?

33

4. Most of your friends and acquaintances don't know how bad the drinking problem is. Why?
5. Why did you feel especially hopeful about your spouse's last attempt to stop drinking? What was the result?
6. What advice did your parents give you?

In class

3. Retell

Members of the class may volunteer to retell the different steps in the development of this dilemma. Each step must be in the order given in the story. If one step is omitted, other students should provide it. One student may list the steps, numbering them, on the chalkboard. Just list phrases as notes to remind everyone of the **chronology** of the events.

order in which events occurred

4. Rethink

Work with a partner. Explain what you would do in this situation. Then discuss how the variations listed below might affect your decision.

1. You have no children./You have children.
2. Your children are very young./They are teenagers.
3. You have been married for just two years./You have been married for twenty years.
4. Your family and friends think that alcoholism is a scandal and shameful./They think it is an illness that requires help and support.
5. The problem is not drinking; it is gambling/drugs/outside love affairs/wife beating/child abuse.

5. Generalize

Work in small groups. Consider that in some countries divorce is prohibited by religion or custom. In other countries, it is more common and more acceptable. Which, if any, of the following reasons do you feel justify divorce? Can you think of other reasons?

1. The husband is lazy, has lost several jobs and is content to be dependent on relatives and welfare./The wife is lazy and doesn't do her duties as wife and mother.
2. The husband wants his wife to stay home and care for their children full time, while she wants to continue her career./He wants her to go out and get a job, but she wants to stay home./She wants her husband to help more with the house and children, but he doesn't want to.
3. The man and woman don't feel in love anymore; they argue often and want their freedom.
4. One partner wants children and the other doesn't.
5. Both partners want children, but one is unable to have any.
6. One of the partners has left home to be with a lover.
7. One of the partners has become severely mentally ill and is in an institution.
8. One of the partners committed a serious crime and is in prison.
9. The husband went away to war and was reported missing, but there never was proof that he was dead.

6. Role Play

A. Getting Ready

Work with a partner. Plan a conversation about a marriage that has problems. One student may be a person with marital problems who is asking a good friend for advice. The other may be the friend who gives advice. After you have talked about the problem, write down a few ideas to use in the conversation. The conversation should be short, so be clear about the points you want to make.

_____

_____

_____

_____

B. Act It Out

Divide the class in half. Pairs of students can perform their role plays for half of the class, which will give more students the opportunity to present their role plays. Remember to keep them short; a couple of minutes is enough to get your ideas across.

10. I Quit

Does it make sense for a long-term employee to quit his or her job? What's more important—good pay and benefits or good human relations?

Before class

1. Read and Decide

Read the story, imagining that you are in this situation, and decide what you would do.

You hate your job. Because you work for a small to medium-sized company, good relations among the employees is very important. For you, the human relations at work have suddenly **turned sour**.

become very unpleasant

Although you never considered the job to be very interesting, you weren't particularly dissatisfied, either. And there was one hope that made it all seem worthwhile. Your department head was approaching retirement. You were sure that since you had done your work satisfactorily and you were the next in line, the job would be yours. You had waited many years for the position. But then everything seemed to go wrong. You had some minor disagreements with the department head. The company was passing through a **rough** period financially. Then one day you were informed that a new man was being **brought in** to replace your department head, a person who, as a former government official, was thought to have good contacts in the government that could benefit your company. When you met him, you disliked him and knew that he was not the kind of person you could work well with. You want very much to quit and are quite sure that you could get a similar job with another company in the same field.

difficult
hired from outside the company

But you are 42 years old with two children who will be approaching university age in a few years. You've explored the field, and the only jobs available would cause you to lose your seniority and take a cut in pay and benefits. It would also mean, of course, leaving a familiar group of people and starting all over again. Your wife also has **mixed feelings**. While she is concerned about the security of the family, she also wants you to feel satisfied with your job. What will you do?

feelings both for and against

2. Review

Practice answering the questions without looking at the text.

1. How did you feel about your job before?
2. What hope did you have for many years?

3. Why was an outsider hired to replace your department head?
4. How do you feel about the new man?
5. How do you feel about your job now?
6. What factors make you think that it might be unwise to change jobs?

In class

3. Retell

Your teacher may ask some students to think of questions to ask about the situation. Others may volunteer the answers. One student may write brief notes from the answers on the chalkboard.

4. Rethink

Work with a partner. Discuss what you would do in this situation. Then discuss how the variations listed below might affect your decision.

1. You are single/married.
2. You are a man/woman.
3. You have children/no children.
4. You are 25/35/40/50 years old.

payment of money
5. Your company offered a good-sized retirement **incentive** if you wanted to retire early.
6. You already have a good job offer./You don't have any offers yet.

5. Generalize

Work in small groups. Consider that in some countries changing jobs is quite common and doesn't reflect badly on a person. In fact, it may mean that a person is capable, ambitious, and moving up in his/her field. In other countries, people tend to remain with their first employer and those who change jobs several times may be regarded as unreliable or unable to work well in a group. With the members of your group, describe the employment practices in your country and your feelings about them. Which of the following would you consider good reasons for changing jobs? What other reasons can you think of?

1. You don't like your boss or some of your co-workers.
2. You could get a higher salary by changing jobs.
3. Your company is in financial difficulty and may **go bankrupt**.
4. You want a **change of pace**.
5. Your family wants you to find a job that would let you spend more time at home, as you now work until fairly late most evenings.
6. Your employer wants to transfer you to a place where you don't want to go.
7. You strongly disagree with some action or policy of your employer.

fail, collapse
some variety, a new
routine

6. Role Play

A. Getting Ready

quitting

Work in small groups to plan a discussion between an employee who is unhappy with the way things are going in the company. He/she likes the boss, but is seriously considering **resigning**. He/she really doesn't think that the boss can do much about the problems, but it makes sense to have a serious talk about it. Decide what the situation is. Members of the group may take one role or the other. Those who will be the boss may work together to offer ways to solve the problems, and explain how the boss will go about it. Those who will be the employee may work together to consider clear and objective ways to present the problems to the boss. Write down a few ideas to use in the presentation. Then choose one person from your group to perform the employee's role in the role play, and one person to be the boss.

_____

_____

_____

_____

B. Act It Out

The two members of each group will perform the role play for the class. If there is time, you may want to have a general class discussion of other ways that the employee or the boss might have handled the situations.

11. Yes Sir, Yes Ma'am

Most people agree that children should obey their parents, but is there a limit? When should kids follow their own inclinations, rather than their parents' advice?

Before class

1. Read and Decide

Read each situation below. Rank them as follows:
1 = The child should definitely obey his or her parents.
2 = The child should perhaps obey, depending on the circumstances.
3 = The child should not be required to obey.

Loud Music

_____ You love popular music. To feel the rhythm and get into the mood of the music, you think it is important to have the volume turned up high. Your parents, however, don't like pop music and have told you to turn the volume way down.

Part-time Job

_____ You have a part-time job in order to have money to do things with your friends and buy yourself some clothes and records. Lately, your parents have been worrying out loud about the high cost of your older brother's education. You know they would like you to contribute some of your money to help pay for it.

Get Married?

_____ You have met someone you really like and are thinking of getting married. Your parents say that you are too young, and they don't approve because the girl/boy is from a different background and social class. They tell you to stop seeing each other.

The Family Business

_____ Your parents own a small family business. They say that since you are sixteen now you should help out by working there in your spare time. You don't want to, because it would take time away from your studies and would leave you almost no chance to do things with your friends. Your parents say that since you get the benefits of the income from the business, you should take some of the responsibility for contributing to it.

Your Clothes

_____ Your hair style and clothes are the same as your friends'. Your parents, however, say you look messy and ridiculous. They tell you to start dressing and grooming yourself more respectably.

Your Career

_____ For years your parents have expected that you would follow in their footsteps and go into business. But all your life you have loved music, and you want to make it your life work. Now that you are at the age to find a job, your parents advise against a music career because music isn't practical or a secure kind of work. They say it would be good to continue music as a hobby.

Poor Grades

_____ Your parents don't approve of your friends. When your last report card showed that some of your grades had dropped, they said it was the bad influence of your friends. You admit that some of your friends aren't very interested in school, but you believe that your grades were low because of a couple of tough, new teachers. But your parents advise you to find new friends. They also want you to limit the time you spend with your old friends until your grades improve.

In class

2. Retell

Members of the class may volunteer to describe each situation. One student may write the title of each situation on the chalkboard, and just a phrase or two from the description to remind everyone about it. Another student may ask members of the class to raise their hands if they ranked the situation as 1, 2, or 3. Write the tally (total number) on the chalkboard next to each title.

Example: <u>1</u> <u>2</u> <u>3</u>
            1   10   5

Remember: 1 = The child should definitely obey his or her parents.
2 = The child should perhaps obey, depending on the circumstances.
3 = The child should not be required to obey.

3. Rethink

Work with a partner. Compare your ranking of each situation. Explain your answers, especially your feelings about the ones you marked as number 2.

4. Generalize

Work in small groups. Discuss with the members of your group how you would feel in the following circumstances:

1. Would your feelings about the above situations change depending on the age of the child, and whether the child were male or female? If so, how?
2. Explain what you would do in the above situations if you were the parent/the child.

5. Role Play

A. Getting Ready

Divide into groups of three. Decide who will be the mother, the father, and the child. Decide on the age of the child. Choose *one* of the following role plays:

1. The parents want the child to help out at the family store, but the child doesn't want to.
2. The parents don't approve of the child's friends and want their child to find new friends. The child defends his/her friends and the right to choose friends.

Write down some ideas you would use to persuade your child/parent to accept your point of view.

_____

_____

_____

_____

B. Act It Out

Each group may perform its role play for the class. Use your notes, keep to the point, and make your role play short.

PART 2

TOWARD ARGUMENTATION

Introduction

We often find ourselves in situations that present problems in our personal lives, but we have little control over the situations because broader social issues or laws are involved.

- [ ] Should an auto executive expose to the press his company's careless manufacturing practices if his superiors won't stop making unsafe cars?
- [ ] Should schools insist that students wear uniforms?
- [ ] Should a permanently unconscious person's right to die be regulated by law or by the wishes of the patient's family?
- [ ] Should smoking in public be legislated or left to individuals?

In the chapters that follow, these complex problems are presented from two points of view. You will be asked to consider both points of view and identify the principal factors in each argument.

Skills you will develop in Part 2 include:
  Noting key words and phrases that signal major points
  Organizing inductive and deductive arguments
  Studying a thesis and antithesis leading to a synthesis
  Brainstorming, evaluating, and ordering ideas
  Using cause and effect in an argument
  Subordinating information
  Qualifying a familiar idea to support your argument

12. Living with In-Laws

In your country, do married couples live with their in-laws? What are the benefits and disadvantages of this arrangement?

Before class

1. Read and Consider

This letter expresses two points of view about a situation. Read Dolores' letter to Ana asking for advice. Consider the pros (reasons for) and cons (reasons against) of making a decision to move in with her in-laws.

Dear Ana,

My husband's parents have suggested that we live with them, but I don't know whether it's a good idea or not. I'd appreciate any advice you might have.

Of course, we'd save a lot of money, and space would be another important advantage, since they have a larger house. We feel very **cramped** now in our little apartment. I could probably ask them to take care of the children when I went out. Maybe I'd even get a part-time job. I think that living with older people would be a good experience for the children, too, although there might be disagreements about how to raise them. We all get along well, especially his mother and I. And I know they'd enjoy having a full house again, since their youngest child recently left home.

But I'm afraid our lives would change a lot! My husband's mother and I would share the cooking and housework, and I'm sure I would always feel it was "her house" and "her kitchen." One good thing about sharing the work, though, is that there would be less work for each of us to do (unless I had to do it all!). The main thing that concerns me is that we'd lose our privacy and the freedom to use the house as we wanted. I don't know if they would enjoy our friends, for instance. In particular, I guess I'd always feel the need to "be on my best behavior." I don't know if I could ever really relax.

So you see I'm really **torn** about what's best. Another possibility might be to postpone the decision and go visit

lack space, can't move freely

confused

49

them more often—maybe stay with them on weekends. Then we could see how things went. But I did want to ask your advice, since you've been living with your in-laws for several years now.

Sincerely,

Dolores

2. Review

Circle the phrases in favor of moving in with the in-laws. Underline the phrases against it.

In class

3. Retell

Your teacher may ask for volunteers to summarize the arguments for and against moving in with the in-laws. One student may list brief phrases on the chalkboard under the two headings "For" and "Against" to help everyone remember the points.

4. Analyze the Content

Work with a partner. Discuss the following questions:

1. How does Dolores feel about her mother-in-law? Quote from the text to support your opinion.
2. Which of these pros and cons seem most important to Dolores? Why?
3. Does Dolores indicate which decision she's likely to make?

5. Analyze the Structure: Key Words

Your teacher will lead the class in discussing the structure of the arguments presented in the letter. Ideas are sometimes, but not always, introduced by key words. Working together, complete the outline below. The key words are provided to help you.

1. Reasons for living together
   a. Of course,

   _____

   b. another important advantage

   _____

   c. could probably ask

   _____

   d. Maybe I'd even

   _____

   e. good experience

   _____

   f. especially

   _____

   g. they'd enjoy

   _____

2. Reasons for not living together
   a. although

   _____

   b. But

   _____

   c. I'm sure

   _____

   d. unless

   _____

   e. concerns me

   _____

f. . . . for instance

_____

g. In particular

_____

In this letter, most of the reasons for living together are given in the second paragraph, and the reasons for living separately are in the third. However, there is one reason for living separately in paragraph 2, and one for living together in paragraph 3. What are they? Why do you think the writer put them there?

6. Generalize

Work in small groups:

1. Discuss the advantages and disadvantages of "nuclear families" (families in which the married children live apart from their parents) versus those of "extended families" (living together). Consider these effects from the point of view of society as a whole.
2. Consider these living situations from three points of view:
   a. the parents
   b. the married children
   c. their children

7. Role Play

A. Getting Ready

Divide the class in half. Each group will plan a skit (short play). A young husband or wife is asking advice from his/her in-laws' other married children. Some feel strongly that the young family should move in with the in-laws; the others argue that it is not a good idea.

Everyone in the group can participate. One person will be the person asking advice. The other students will be in favor of it, or against it. Write down a few ideas for your role in the skit.

_____

_____

_____

_____

B. Act It Out

Each group may present its skit for the other half of the class. At the end of the skit, the person asking advice must make a decision about the move.

13. An Explosive Situation

If your company were manufacturing an unsafe product for public use, would you risk your job to get your employer to correct the problem?

Before class

1. Read and Consider

Read the following exchange of memos between a concerned automobile manufacturing executive and his/her supervisor.

To: J. Simmons   From: R. Klein

Subject: Fuel Tank Design   Date: January 9
        on the XTP

I've just seen the new design of the XTP. I strongly urge you to authorize safety tests on the fuel tank of the new XTP car before putting it on the market. I realize that the designers relocated the fuel tank in order to reduce the car's size and weight, but its present position makes it likely to explode in a collision. We don't want to be responsible for injuries.

To: R. Klein   From: J. Simmons

Subject: Memo of 1/9   Date: March 16

I shared your concern about the XTP's fuel tank with the design engineers recently. They say many safety tests have been conducted already and that the chances of the gas tank's exploding in a collision are no greater for the XTP than they are for any other car. If we were to change the location of the gas tank, we'd have to increase the weight and price of the car. The tests you propose would also cost the company a tremendous amount of time and money. My decision at this time is to do no further tests.

54

To: J. Simmons   From: R. Klein

Subject: Fuel Tank Testing   Date: December 2
          on the XTP

Since we started production last summer, I've read about three accidents involving the XTP. In every case, the fuel tank exploded and passengers were burned. I can't dismiss these cases as coincidences. I believe that the existing safety tests, which were conducted before the relocation of the fuel tank, were inadequate.

I've reached the point where I can't work here any longer with a clear conscience unless the situation changes. If you are unwilling to authorize safety tests on the XTP fuel tank within the next six months, I will resign. I will also consider sharing my knowledge with the press.

cc: S. Lawler, President

2. Review

What is the main point of each memo?

In class

3. Retell

One student may read each of the following questions aloud. Members of the class may volunteer the answers. If an answer is incomplete, other students should contribute.

1. Why is Klein concerned about the design of the XTP?
2. Why was the fuel tank relocated?
3. What's wrong with the position of the fuel tank?
4. What action did Simmons take in response to Klein's memo?
5. Does Simmons agree with Klein? Why or why not? Give four reasons.
6. What is Simmons' decision?

7. What new information strengthens (adds weight to) Klein's position?
8. What is Klein's final proposal?

4. Analyze the Content

Work with a partner to analyze the arguments presented in the memos. Together, prepare a response to each item and fill in the blanks.

Each memo contains a main position that the speaker wishes to argue and details that support it. The main position answers the question, "What does he/she want?" The supporting details answer the question, "Why?"

> Example:
> January 9 memo
> Main position: Simmons should authorize safety tests on the XTP's fuel tank.
>
> Supporting details:
>   1. The XTP may explode in a collision.
>   2. We don't want to be responsible for injuries.

Briefly summarize the main position and supporting details for the other two memos.

March 16 memo

Main position: _____

Supporting details:

    1. _____

    2. _____

    3. _____

    4. _____

December 2 memo

Main position: _____

Supporting details:

    1. _____

    2. _____

5. Analyze the Structure: Deductive and Inductive Arguments

Work as a class with your teacher to analyze the structure of deductive and inductive arguments.

A. Deductive Arguments

Deductive arguments begin with a general statement (a fact, a principle, a law, etc.) and proceed to specific statements that follow logically from the general premise.

Example: General statement: Drunk driving is the cause of many unnecessary road deaths.

Resulting deductions:

1. Therefore each driver should exercise self-control and not drive after drinking.
2. Therefore traffic laws should severely punish drunk drivers in order to deter future drunk driving.
3. Therefore driver education courses should teach that alcohol and driving don't mix.

Note: The sequencing of the ideas does not alter their logical relationship. Therefore the above deductive argument can take two forms while remaining deductive:

1. main statement,   therefore   1,2,3
$\longrightarrow$

2. 1, 2, 3   because   main statement
$\longleftarrow$

B. Inductive Arguments

Inductive arguments begin with specific observations and proceed to a general conclusion that logically follows from those specific observations.

Example: Specific Observations:

1. The patient has a fever.
2. His bones and joints ache.
3. He feels exhausted.

Conclusion: He probably has influenza.

Note: The sequencing of the ideas does not alter their logical relationship. Therefore the above inductive argument can take two forms while remaining inductive:

1. 1, 2, 3   therefore   general conclusion
$\longrightarrow$

2. general conclusion   because   1, 2, 3
$\longleftarrow$

C. Check the Reading

The memos about the XTP all illustrate the same type of reasoning. Do you think they are deductive or inductive?

6. Practice

Work with a partner. Read each argument below. In each blank, write **D** if you think the argument is Deductive, and **I** if you think it is Inductive.

_____ 1. Our company's policy is to provide consumers with safe, reliable vehicles. Therefore, we conduct thorough safety tests at all stages of design and production. We also are willing to recall vehicles for modification if there appears to be a defect.

_____ 2. Many children die because they lack proper nutrition, safe drinking water and inoculations against preventable diseases.

_____ 3. The grass is turning green, the wind has lost its cold bite, and the buds are swelling. Everything around us proclaims the arrival of spring.

_____ 4. I'm going to pack my bags, leave no forwarding address, and take off on a long, leisurely trip because I need to rethink my whole life.

7. Generalize

Work in small groups to discuss the following questions. Consider that concern for the public welfare can sometimes conflict with feelings of loyalty to one's employer and the desire to protect one's own security.

1. Which do you think is more important: loyalty to one's company, to one's security, or to public safety?
2. Do you think that it's enough to resign from a job that involves deceiving the public, or do you think that it's also necessary to alert the public?

8. Role Play

A. Getting Ready

Work with a partner and choose *one* of the situations below for a role play. Practice your role-play with your partner.

newspapers, TV, magazines, radio

a solution that both sides can agree on

1. Act out the conversation that follows the exchange of memos about the XTP, when the boss (J. Simmons) asks the executive (R. Klein) for a private meeting. The executive wants to keep his/her job if possible, but nonetheless threatens to go to the **press** if the company doesn't do something about the dangerous car. Try to come to some **mutually acceptable solution**.

change his/her mind

2. Act out a conversation between the concerned executive and his/her spouse. The executive explains the dilemma and says that he/she has decided to quit the company and talk to the press. The spouse tries to **talk him/her out of it** and find some other acceptable course of action.

B. Act It Out

You may be asked to present your role-play for the class.

14. Should Smoking Be Banned in Public?

In your country, is smoking banned in some public places? Do you feel that the decision whether or not to smoke in public should be made by the smoker or by law?

Before class

1. Read and Consider

Read this essay, which balances both positions, and consider what reasonable conclusion could be made.

refer to, present

Some people feel that smoking should be banned in public. The arguments supporting this belief vary considerably. Some people **cite** medical research stating that smoke exhaled by smokers is more harmful to nonsmokers, especially children and old people, than it is to the smokers themselves. Others argue that there are laws against drinking in public, and so there should be similar laws against smoking. The smell of smoke makes some people feel sick. In a restaurant, smoke affects the taste of other diners' food. Cigarette butts discarded in public are often

ugly sight
danger

an **eyesore** or a fire **hazard**. When a lighted cigarette is dropped on a carpet, chair, or table, it can damage the article and leave an ugly burn mark. Much sidewalk litter consists of smokers' discards, such as butts and empty packages. In crowded areas, smokers sometimes accidentally burn other people's clothes.

strongly

But there are people who **vehemently** defend their right to smoke wherever they want. Smoking is a personal matter, they say, and no more dangerous or harmful than driving a car or crossing a street. Should the law prevent them from doing these things? Many people also smoke as a

pressure, anxiety

way to feel relaxed when under **stress**. Should people who have just experienced some emotional strain (such as students who have just finished a difficult exam) be denied the right to calm their nerves? And what about people who really enjoy the taste of tobacco after a meal?

sweet after-dinner
drink

They argue that smoking a cigarette or pipe is no different from enjoying the taste of a rich pastry or an expensive **liqueur**. But for many smokers,

60

disturb, regulate

the most important question is whether the government has the right to **interfere** in a person's personal life. Is it the government's responsibility to tell individual citizens what they can and cannot do in public?

discussion without reason

This problem is a difficult one that can easily be reduced to **emotionalism**. Whichever position you support, do you think there is a reasonable solution to the problem?

2. Review

Close your book and try to remember the main points for and against banning smoking in public places.

In class

3. Retell

Your teacher may call on students to add to the list of arguments used by smokers and nonsmokers. One student may list the points on the chalkboard.

Nonsmokers	**Smokers**
1. Smoke is more harmful to children and old people than it is to smokers.	1. Smoking is a personal matter.
2.	2.
3.	3.
4.	4.

4. Analyze the Content

Work with a partner in this exercise. Notice that the writer of this essay uses several analogies to strengthen the arguments. An *analogy* is a comparison between two things that is used to illustrate a point. Often, analogies use the word "like."

> Example: If the teacher corrected every little mistake I made, I'd become nervous. *That's like* trying to learn how to ski and always worrying about falling down.

If the objects of comparison are very similar, the analogy is considered "fair"; if they have obvious differences, the analogy is unfair. The following statement is an example of an unfair analogy: Wearing a uniform to school is exactly like being in the army.

Work with your partner to find three examples of analogies in the essay on smoking. List the similarities and differences between the ideas being compared. The first one is partially done for you.

1. Smoking in public is like drinking in public.
   Similarities
   a. Smoking and drinking can both be objectionable if overdone.

   b. _____

   c. _____
   Differences
   a. Too much alcohol can make the drinker violent, but smoking doesn't change the personality.

   b. _____

   c. _____
   Is the analogy fair?

2. _____
   Similarities
   a. _____

   b. _____

   c. _____
   Differences

   a. _____

   b. _____

   c. _____

Is the analogy fair?

3. _____

Similarities

a. _____

b. _____

c. _____

Differences

a. _____

b. _____

c. _____

Is the analogy fair?

5. Analyze the Structure: Thesis, Antithesis, Synthesis

Work as a class with your teacher to analyze the structure of the essay on smoking. Notice that there are three parts to the essay:

1. Thesis: the first position. Summarize it.
2. Antithesis: the second position. Summarize it.
3. Synthesis: the conclusion, which attempts to resolve the argument. Summarize it.

Each part is complete in itself, uninterrupted by elements from the other two. Does this organization work well? Is it a balanced presentation? Look at the lists of factors on the board under the headings "Nonsmokers" and "Smokers."

1. Does the pro-smoking section address the non-smoking arguments?
2. Does the non-smoking section address the pro-smoking arguments?
3. Do you think this organization is as effective as presenting one point at a time for each side?
4. In what situations would this kind of structure work best? Name as many possibilities as you can.

6. Practice

Work with a partner. Look again at the readings in Chapters 12 and 13. Take turns summarizing the thesis, antithesis, and conclusion for each chapter. Try to come to agreement on the summary statement for the three parts of each argument.

7. Generalize

Work in small groups to discuss the following:

1. To what extent are you *for* or *against* banning smoking in public? If you are *for* banning it, how do you think it should be carried out?
2. Can you think of other controversial subjects that some people would like to deal with by law? Take a quick vote in your group about reaction to any of the ideas.

8. Role Play

A. Getting Ready

Work in small groups. Half of the students in each group can represent nonsmokers in your workplace. The other half can represent smokers. About 60 percent of the people in your workplace smoke. The nonsmokers think that majority rule is not appropriate here. Write down a few notes for your argument. Try to use analogies.

_____

_____

_____

_____

B. Act It Out

Practice your role play in your group. Try to reach a reasonable compromise. Then one group may perform it a second time for the whole class.

15. Let Her Die

If your relative had a bad accident and the doctors said she'd never regain consciousness, would you want her to be allowed to die? Do you think that families should be able to make this decision when the patient can't?

Before class

1. Read and Consider

The following is a conversation between two friends of the family of an accident victim who is unlikely to recover. Consider their opinions.

A: She lies in the hospital bed day after day, unconscious. Her husband and children visit, but she has never regained consciousness. The accident turned her into a **vegetable**.

a living thing with no mental activity, feelings, or ability to communicate or move

B: Do the doctors think there's any chance of recovery?

A: No, they say her brain was badly damaged. They expect her to stay unconscious until she dies. In fact, she probably wouldn't be able to stay alive at all if the hospital didn't have special equipment to keep her breathing. With the equipment, though, they think she might live for years.

B: You mean that if the doctors just unplugged the machine, it would solve the problem?

A: She would probably die, if that's what you mean by "solve the problem." That would be murder, though, of course.

B: I don't know. I suppose you could say that she actually died at the time of the accident. She's not alive now in the sense of feeling anything or knowing what's happening. I'd say that if there really is no hope for her, the doctors should think about her family. The pain of this "living death" and the huge expense of the medical care is too much for them to bear year after year.

A: But that's a big "if." If they wait, maybe the doctors will find a way to help her. Or maybe there will be a miracle. I think that human life is sacred. We have no right to decide when it is over.

zero
continue

B: Oh, come on. The chances of either of those things happening are **nil**. Doctors know enough now to **prolong** people's pain and suffering even when they can't cure the disease. To me, that's cruel, not merciful.

set the limit
saying that mercy is the reason

A: It may be more merciful in some cases to let people die, but where do you **draw the line**? Rather than just letting death come naturally, people will start killing **in the name of "mercy."** Some people will be tempted to kill for selfish reasons—to inherit money or to avoid caring for a hopelessly ill person.

B: Well, perhaps you're right. It's a terrible dilemma. I really feel sorry for the woman's family.

2. Review

Most people have an immediate emotional response to this topic. Determine what yours is, and then try to restate, objectively, the points made for both sides of the argument.

In class

3. Retell

Volunteers may complete one of the following sentences by writing it on the chalkboard. If there is space on the chalkboard, more than one person can be writing at a time. Do all members of the class agree that the sentences are completed correctly?

1. The speakers are discussing . . .
2. The patient's condition is serious because . . .
3. The doctors predict . . .
4. The equipment that keeps her breathing is important because . . .
5. **A** thinks that the machine should stay plugged in because . . .
6. **B** thinks it might be better to unplug the machine because . . .

4. Analyze the Content

Work with a partner and discuss the dialog.

1. Consider that the two people in the dialog seem to have different concepts of what "life" means. One of you may describe **A**'s concept, based on the comments made. The other may describe **B**'s concept.
2. **B** thinks that unplugging the machine would solve the problem. What does **A** think about **B**'s solution?
3. After **A** says that unplugging the machine would be murder, **B** says, "I don't know," which is a mild way of disagreeing. In conversations like this, the second person often follows this kind of comment with a counterargument. What is **B**'s counterargument?
4. **A** says, "But that's a big 'if'." What does "if" refer to?
5. "Oh, come on" is a stronger way of disagreeing. It means "Don't be silly," or "What you're saying is foolish." What is another possible expression for disagreeing more strongly?

6. **B** says, "The chances of either of those things happening are nil." What are "those things"?
7. In **B**'s opinion, what is cruel? **A** seems to agree partially, saying that "It may be more merciful in some cases." Actually, **A** is saying, "Your point is only a half-truth. It may be true in some cases, but usually, it's not." **A** then makes a counterpoint. What is it? What examples does **A** give?
8. One friendly way to end a discussion like this is to agree on some point, even if it's not the main issue under discussion. What point do **A** and **B** agree on?

5. Analyze the Structure: Brainstorming, Evaluating, and Ordering Ideas

Work as a class with your teacher to analyze the preparation of a more formal argument than the one in the dialog. Use the topic of the dialog as an example.

When we argue informally, we often include information and opinions that aren't necessary to our argument. Or we may use relevant ideas and information but state them out of order. This is especially common when many people are involved in the conversation, and points are ignored and must be reintroduced.

When we prepare a formal speech or document (such as a report or editorial), however, it is best to eliminate irrelevant material and order our thoughts meaningfully. An important first step in preparing a formal argument is to *brainstorm*. That means quickly writing down all your ideas on a subject without attention to order or style. For example, if **B** decided to write a letter to the local newspaper in favor of mercy killing, his/her brainstorming notes might look something like this:

_____ She's a vegetable.

_____ No hope of recovery—brain badly damaged.

_____ I knew her before the accident.

_____ Doctors could solve problem by unplugging equipment.

_____ Equipment could keep her alive for years.

_____ She had such a happy childhood.

_____ She can't feel anything; doesn't know what's going on.

_____ The family can't afford to pay her hospital bills forever.

_____ It's cruel to prolong suffering when there's no cure.

_____ Some people believe "While there's life there's hope"—I disagree.

6. Practice

1. Now work with a partner to decide which of these notes should *not* be included in the letter to the editor. Draw a line through them. Number the remaining notes in the order in which you think they should appear.
2. Compare your order with that of your classmates. Members of the class may volunteer to read sentence 1, then 2, and so on. If you disagree, explain your point of view.

7. Generalize

Work in small groups. Discuss the following situation.

Should surgery be performed on a newborn baby who has a breathing problem?

The infant was born badly deformed physically and probably also mentally. The baby will die if the breathing problem isn't corrected immediately by surgery. What if the parents are wealthy/middle class/ poor? How will the costs be handled? How should the costs be handled in cases when the parents want the operation, but can't possibly pay for it? Consider the larger problem for society if "medical miracles" are demanded, but there is no government aid to absorb the cost.

8. Role Play

A. Getting Ready

Work in small groups. Decide which members of the group will role-play the patient, the doctor, and the patient's family members. (Family members must represent both the pro and con sides.) The patient is elderly, and is being kept alive by medicine. His/her health is bad, and there is no joy in life. Lately, he/she has been refusing food and trying to refuse the medication. As you prepare for the role play, write down a few notes for your role in the conference with the family, the patient, and the doctor about what's to be done. Number the points in the order in which you want to express them. Can you make a strong argument in favor of the patient's right to decide? Can you persuade him/her to want to live?

_____

_____

_____

_____

B. Act It Out

You are all seated around the patient. Begin your role play.

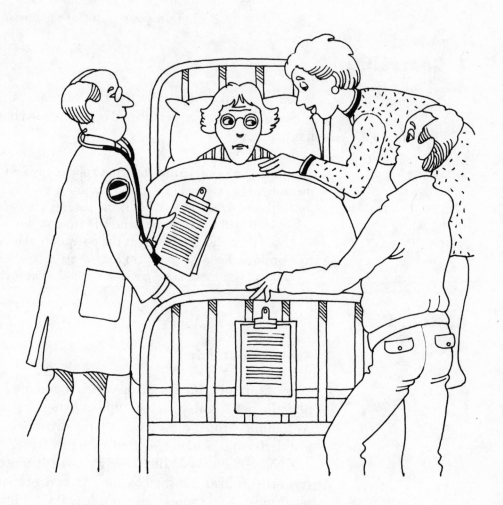

16. Uniforms

Have you ever had to wear a uniform? How did you feel? Often, institutions like them better than the individuals who have to wear them.

Before class

1. Read and Consider

Read the following discussion between a student and teacher at a secondary school. Is there a right and wrong side in this argument, or merely two points of view?

A: Why do we have to wear uniforms to school? Why can't we wear ordinary clothes, like kids at some schools?

B: You know the rules. The school feels that if students dress conservatively, they will act properly and be more serious about their studies. Personally, I think they have a point there.

small parts

A: Well, maybe, but at the same time it makes us all feel like **cogs** in a machine. We can't be creative or express ourselves in our own way. That's important, too, isn't it?

B: I wouldn't disagree with that, but we mustn't forget the majority of students. When students can dress any way they want, that can

disturb

sometimes **disrupt** the classroom, and make it difficult for some students to study. The main purpose of school is to study, not to

display

show off your clothes.

A: Why does someone else always have to decide what is good for the majority? Why doesn't anyone ever ask us what we think? We should be able to make some of our own decisions.

B: When you are eighteen you can make your own decisions. Right now, your main responsibility is to study hard and learn how to cooperate with your fellow students.

A: Are you saying that if I don't wear a uniform I won't study hard and cooperate with my fellow students?

You are saying something I didn't say at all.

B: No, **you're putting words in my mouth**. I'm only trying to say that the school feels that wearing uniforms will help prevent some

purpose

unnecessary problems. Their **intention** is not to discourage creativity or free thinking.

A: Maybe that's what you believe, but we are the ones who have to wear them. Lots of kids feel that the school makes us wear uniforms to try to mold us into thinking in the same way. I don't want to become just one more **faceless number** in society.

an individual without an identity

2. Review

Close your book and try to remember the arguments **A** expresses. Open your book and check them. Do the same for **B**.

In class

3. Retell

Look at the points listed for **A** and **B** in the boxes below. Find the sentence in the dialog that represents each factor. One student may read the factor. Members of the class may volunteer to read the sentence in the dialog.

A	B
1. look-alike feeling	1. school policy
2. passive atmosphere prevents free thought and creativity	2. people act the way they dress
3. decisions made without consulting students	3. majority is important
4. clothes do not determine how much a person studies	4. to dress any way you want may interfere with classroom atmosphere
5. shapes students' thinking	5. study more important than clothes
	6. some problems can be avoided
	7. school's purpose is not to stifle creative thought

4. Analyze the Content

Work with a partner and describe the speakers of the dialog. One of you may describe **A**, and the other may describe **B**. Now examine the list of adjectives below that describe the teacher and the student. Discuss each one and decide whether that word fits **A** or **B**. Write **A** or **B** next to the word. Find comments from the dialog to support your choices. You may want to add some additional words of your own.

_____ Flexible

_____ Rigid

_____ Opinionated

_____ Concerned

_____ Easy-going

_____ Cautious

_____ Stuffy

_____ Conservative

_____ Excited

_____ _____

_____ _____

_____ _____

5. Analyze the Structure: Cause and Effect

Work as a class with your teacher to analyze the structure of a cause-and-effect argument. It is a common way to organize a logical argument. This form of organization has three parts:

**having contradictory
qualities**

1. The speaker or writer states the central concern, with its interesting, startling, or **paradoxical** aspects.
2. The speaker or writer asks and answers the question, "Why."
3. The speaker or writer suggests solutions.

Example

1. Central concern: A new local restaurant requires men to wear coats and ties, and women to be "appropriately dressed." Although a lot of customers like the "dressed-up" atmosphere of the place, there have also been a lot of complaints.

2. Why? Many people prefer casual clothes. It suits their lifestyle. As long as they are dressed neatly, they say, why can't they enjoy the good food, too, without the discomfort and bother of getting "dressed up"?

3. Solution: The owner might consider adding on a small, informal café. Then the customers would have a choice, and the owner would attract a much larger crowd for dinner every evening. The extra investment would certainly be worth it.

6. Practice

Work with a partner in this exercise. The high school student in the dialog about uniforms has decided to write an article for the school paper. He/she hopes to persuade the school board and the administration to be more flexible. Complete the outline for the article.

1. Central concern: Most members of the school board support the rule requiring students to wear uniforms. However, most students do not.

2. Why?

   School board members want students to wear uniforms because (three reasons):

   _____

   _____

   _____

   Students object to wearing uniforms because (four reasons):

   _____

   _____

   _____

   _____

3. Suggested solution: _____

Now compare your solution with that of your classmates. One member of each pair may read his or her suggestions.

7. Generalize

Work in small groups. Discuss whether **B**'s arguments for uniforms would make sense if applied to other groups (for example, police officers, service men and women, convicts, youth groups such as the scouts, beauticians, and fire fighters). What other reasons are there for wearing uniforms?

8. Role Play

A. Getting Ready

Work in small groups to plan a role play about a dispute between workers and management over a dress code. At present, the company forbids wearing certain kinds of clothes for safety, morale, and productivity reasons.

Half of your group will represent management, and half the employees. The employees will try to persuade the management to change their policy. The management must explain the reasons for the policy. They may change the policy a little if the points presented are reasonable.

Write down a few notes for your role.

_____

_____

_____

_____

B. Act It Out

Perform the employee/management role play. Be persuasive, but not angry or forceful. You want good results, not just the chance to voice your complaints.

17. The Sunshine Law

The sunshine law states that no building may be erected that robs an existing building of sunlight.

Before class

1. Read and Consider

an official document giving permission to build

prevent

space

one level, floor

to be the first person on a piece of land

bother, disturb

situation

Dear Editor:

I have been trying to build a new house for the last year and a half, but the neighbor across the street has prevented me from getting a **building permit**. She says that the house would **block out** the sunshine in front of her house in the morning. The garden in front of her house is her greatest pleasure, she says. It seems a bit strange that a person who already lives in a nice, big house and has a garden would prevent a neighbor from building a much-needed bigger house.

My four children are all in school and need more **room** for studying. Also, my parents are old, and are going to come and live with us. We are now living in a **one-story** house that has four rooms and a bath, and it just is not big enough for everyone.

I can understand her feelings, and I wish I had enough time in the morning to sit in the sunshine and look at flowers. My children have grown up in this neighborhood. Do you think that they want to move away from their friends or have to enter another school? Should I be denied the basic right to a minimum standard of living?

The **right of first domain** may be justifiable in some cases; but in the crowded world we live in today, it does not seem realistic to **interfere with** another person's basic standard of living.

I have presented my **case** to the city government, but they say they can't do anything because of the sunshine law. My other neighbors think that I should take the case

to court to get the permit, but that would cost a lot of
money.
   What do you think about this situation? Do you think
the sunshine law should be **strictly** applied in my case?

Sincerely,

A man in need of a bigger house

**without compromise,
exactly**

2. Review

Put yourself in the place of the writer of the letter. What are your
reasons for wanting an exception to the sunshine law made for you?
What are the rights of the woman across the street? Why are her
rights especially important to her?

In class

3. Retell

One student may write the heading "Man in Need of Bigger House,"
on the chalkboard. He/she may write notes of responses to each of
the factors listed under the heading "Neighbor" below. Your teacher
may ask students to respond to each factor under "Neighbor" from
the letter-writer's point of view.

Neighbor	**Man in Need of Bigger House**
1. right of first domain 2. lack of sunshine would affect plants 3. wouldn't be able to enjoy morning sunshine 4. man can move to another place 5. sunshine law guarantees right to sunshine	

4. Analyze the Content

Work with a partner. Look at the list of factors listed in the previous exercise. Many of the writer's points are expressed directly (his reasons for wanting more room, for example). He is less direct in dealing with his neighbor's points. He uses sarcasm or irony (saying the opposite of what is meant, in a critical way). Discuss your answers to the following questions.

1. What does the writer really mean in the following sentences?
   a. It seems a bit strange that a person who already lives in a nice, big house and has a garden would prevent a neighbor from building a much-needed bigger house.
   b. I can understand her feelings and wish I had enough time in the morning to look at flowers.
2. Some points are presented in the form of rhetorical questions (questions for which the letter-writer already has answers). He's seeking agreement here, not information. Find two rhetorical questions in his letter.

_____

_____

Compare your answers with those of your classmates. Your teacher may ask a few students to give their answers to each of the questions.

Example:

I. _____
   A. _____
   B. _____
II. _____

5. Analyze the Structure: Subordinating Information

Work with your teacher as a class. Identify subordinating information for the main points of the argument presented by the neighbor who won't allow the building permit. What are the facts and opinions that support the main points?

Decide together which of the points listed below are main points and which are supporting facts or opinions.

I lived in the neighborhood first.
My morning pleasure would be gone without my garden.
I built the garden so that I could sit and enjoy the sun.

I think my neighbor should move if he needs a bigger house.

I've got the right of first domain.

I don't want my neighbor to get a building permit.

The addition to his house would block my sunshine.

dry up, decay   Without the sun, my garden would **wither**.

I saved for years in order to be able to move from a drab, dark apartment overlooking an alley to this nice, sunny house.

My neighbor says that he needs more room.

My neighbor says that a person's basic standard of living is more important than the right of first domain.

6. Practice

Work with a partner to put the main points and supporting information of the argument into outline form. Use Roman numerals for the main points (I, II, III, etc.) and capital letters for the supporting details (A, B, C).

7. Generalize

Work in small groups. Describe a law in your country; give one or two main points and supporting details, either in support of or against the law.

8. Role Play

A. Getting Ready

Choose a person from your group to act out the role of someone expressing his/her feelings about a law from your group discussion (or a U.S. law). Select another person to present the opposite point of view. Help each person prepare for the role with main points and supporting details. Write a few notes and offer them to the actors. Try to be reasonable and persuasive, as these two people are neighbors and must continue to live in harmony.

_____

_____

_____

_____

B. Act It Out

The role plays can be presented for the whole class.

18. Stronger Government Control of Population Needed

In your country, is birth control a matter for individuals to decide for themselves, or does the government try to influence that decision?

Before class

1. Read and Consider

Read this editorial for one point of view.

openly state one's opinion

come from two causes that are equally important

good, worthy of praise

Following the government's recent official report on population control, the editors of the *Morning Telegraph* feel it is time for us to **take a stand** on this important yet difficult matter. The report states that the rate of population growth is still unacceptably high. We agree. We also agree with the report's outline of the causes of this high growth rate, causes that **are rooted as much in** our cultures and traditions **as in** a lack of information and resources. We would, however, cite one more major cause— the failure of the government to take strong enough measures.

While we respect the basic right of adults to decide family matters for themselves, we feel that the dangers of uncontrolled population growth are unacceptable. The government's efforts in public education and persuasion have been **commendable** but, unfortunately, insufficient. People's attitudes must be changed. Although we feel that stronger measures are undesirable, we believe they can no longer be avoided. The country must commit itself to actively encouraging small families. Money should be made available for educational assistance and medical care for first and second children. Government housing should be limited to two-child families. The government should discourage the promotion of any civil servant having more than three children.

When our rate of economic growth rises significantly above our rate of population growth, people's lives will improve, and then—as has been the pattern in other countries—people will desire fewer children. Until that time, we must all make some sacrifices.

2. Review

Consider whether you agree with the points made in the editorial.

In class

3. Retell

One student may read the questions below aloud, and select volunteers who wish to answer them.

1. Whose opinion is explained in this article?
2. What is the main idea of the article?
3. What is the government's policy on population control, according to the article?
4. Is the author basically agreeing or basically disagreeing with the government's population policies?
5. What population policy does the author propose?

4. Analyze the Content

Work with a partner. Reread the following sentences:

1. "While we respect the basic right of adults to decide family matters for themselves, we feel that the dangers of uncontrolled population growth are unacceptable."
2. "Although we feel that stronger measures are undesirable, we believe they can no longer be avoided."

Each sentence has two ideas that conflict with each other. The writer thinks that both ideas are true, but in each case one idea is more important than the other. In each sentence, underline the idea that the writer considers more important. Do the words "while" and "although" introduce the more important idea or the secondary one? Find one more example of this kind of sentence.

5. Analyze the Structure: Qualification of a Familiar Idea

Work as a class with your teacher to analyze the structure of this argument's presentation. Typically, the first part of such an argument will confirm a familiar idea, the second part will state a qualification or objection, and the third will draw a balanced conclusion. Notice how the key words in the editorial progress through the three steps.

agree (signaling area of agreement)
also agree (another point of agreement)
however, cite one more (expanding the position)
while (qualifying) . . . *we feel* (personal opinion)
although (qualifying) . . . *we feel* (personal opinion)
must (strong opinion)
should (recommendation)
should (recommendation)
should (recommendation)
when (stating a condition) . . . *and then* (effect)
until that time (stating duration of a condition)

6. Practice

Work with a partner. Go back to the editorial and circle each word
from the list above and then underline the point following it.

7. Generalize

Work in small groups. Discuss the following questions:

1. Should individual freedom, or the freedom of couples, be deter-
   mined by the government in the case of family planning?
2. Do you agree with the opinion that overpopulation is the cause
   of poverty in less developed countries? What other factors are
   important? List, in order of importance, the factors that you feel
   contribute most directly to poverty and hunger.
3. What factors cause family planning efforts to be more successful
   in some countries than in others?

8. Role Play

A. Getting Ready

Prepare to role-play a television panel discussion on the subject of
population control. World population is now over five billion. Members of the panel include a doctor, a religious leader, a family plan-

ning agency head, and two government officials who will present their points of view. Divide into groups. Select one person from each group to be a panel member. (A different panel member should be chosen by each group.) Help your panel member prepare to present his/her views. Write a few notes and share them with your group.

_____

_____

_____

_____

B. Act It Out

The panel members may present the role play for the class.

PART 3

ARGUMENTATION

Introduction

In the chapters that follow, you will find yourself in situations in which you feel very strongly about a particular point of view or course of action. You will try to persuade others to agree with you. Some of the lessons present everyday situations which reflect moral choices. Others present debates of major social issues. Following are examples of the topics that are included:

☐ Is physical violence ever the way to resolve personal disputes?
☐ You and a colleague disagree about the qualifications of job candidates for a position in your company.
☐ What criteria are most important in resolving the conflict over saving endangered species?
☐ What are the social costs of increasing military spending?

Skills you will develop in Part 3 include:
Stating possibilities and exceptions
Raising objections
Introducing supporting evidence or examples
Bringing the discussion back to your point or the major point
Discounting or minimizing the other person's point
Challenging directly and indirectly
Stating opinions
Expressing disbelief and doubt
Using the speaker's previous point to strengthen your argument
Avoiding overgeneralizations

19. Someone Stole My Sandwiches

When we're children, our parents usually teach us to try to settle arguments with words, not fists. Is fighting ever more effective?

Before class

1. Read and Evaluate

Read this discussion between two brothers and decide what you would do. Notice how they express their opinions in informal English.

bother, provoke
boy/man

A: Why are you so quiet? Somebody **give you a hard time** at school?
B: Some **guy** in my class stole the sandwiches out of my lunchbox.
A: Do you know who it was?
B: Yeah. He's done the same thing to some other kids, but everyone is afraid to say anything to him.
A: What did you do?
B: That's the problem. I didn't do anything. I'm not really afraid of the guy, but Dad has always told us that we shouldn't fight unless it's absolutely necessary. What do you think I should have done?

hit
continue doing something wrong without being punished

quite
attack
hurt
frighten

A: Dad's usually right; but in this case if the kid has done it several times before, maybe you should have **punched** him in the nose. If no one does anything, he'll think he can **keep on getting away with it**.
B: I thought of doing that. But that might have made a bigger problem for me. Besides, who knows? Maybe he doesn't have enough money to buy lunch. His clothes do look **pretty** old.
A: Well, you could ask the other kids in your class to help you **jump** him after school. You don't have to **beat** him **up**. Just **give him a good scare**.
B: That might create a problem for some of the smaller kids. He might beat them up later when they are alone. Maybe I'll ask him tomorrow why he took the sandwiches and see what he says.

Impossible!

A: Do you think he's going to admit that he took them? *No way*! If you talk to him, he'll feel that he has to defend himself in front of the other kids. He won't let you make him look bad.
B: Yeah, but I could talk to him alone. I'll tell him that I'm not afraid of him and that we should talk about it and then forget about what he did.

succeed

A: It may **work**, but he'll probably think that you're crazy. Then you'll come home without any teeth. Actually, it's probably too late to do anything; but if it happens again, I'd go up to him and hit him in the nose right away without saying a word. That will surprise him, and he won't bother you or anyone else after that.

deal with
take care of

B: I suppose that *is* one way to **handle** the situation, but it doesn't really **solve** anything.

In class

2. Retell

Students may volunteer to tell parts of the story described in the dialog.

3. Analysis of Content

Work with a partner. Look at the points listed below for **A** and **B**. Find the sentence or sentences in the dialog that contain each factor. Put the number of the factor in the margin of the dialog next to the sentence.

A	B
1. If someone doesn't stop the thief, he'll keep on stealing.	1. Dad says that violence is bad.
2. If a group scares the thief, he may reform.	2. Fighting may create a bigger problem.
3. Scolding the thief in public may force him to defend his image.	3. There may be a good reason for bad behavior.
4. If you try not to fight, you may get hurt.	4. If a group attacks the thief, he may hurt the smaller group members later.
5. Immediate action is important; surprise the person.	5. Talking in private avoids humiliation in public.
	6. Violence doesn't necessarily solve problems.

4. Analysis of Discussion Techniques: Stating a Possibility, Stating an Exception

Work as a class with your teacher to understand these discussion techniques. Two ways of politely expressing an opinion are *stating a possibility* and *stating an exception*. Often these involve the use of conditional verb forms.

Stating a Possibility

Examples: It's quite likely that the workers will go on strike.
If you challenge her, she may/might become angry.
There's always a chance that something good might happen.

What are some examples in the dialog of stating the possibility that something might happen?

Stating an Exception

Examples: In most cases, that would be true, but if . . .
Ninety-nine percent of the time that is what would happen, but this is an exception.
I think there may be some exceptions . . .

What are some examples in the dialog of stating an exception?

5. Practice

Work with a partner. Read sentence 1, below. One of you may restate it as a possibility. Then your partner may try it. Continue with sentence 2.

1. I'm going to quit if I don't get a raise.

                    _____

2. He can't afford to buy lunch.

                    _____

Now work on statements of exception. Read sentence 1, below, state an exception, and make a counterpoint. Express the counterpoint in several different ways, using the various discussion techniques you have studied.

1. Violence always leads to violence.

                    _____

2. Dad says, "If you give a bully an inch, he'll take a mile."

                    _____

6. Discuss

Work in small groups:

1. Discuss the meaning of these sayings. What other phrases do you know in English or in your own language to describe the kind of behavior that is described in this unit? As a parent, what philosophy would you teach your children?

   Might makes right.
   Turn the other cheek.
   An eye for an eye, a tooth for a tooth.
   Do unto others as you would have them do unto you.
   The law of the jungle.
   The survival of the fittest.

2. In everyday life, adults face situations in which a person or group uses physical force or political power or money to gain unfair advantage—in other words, to "bully." Give some specific examples and discuss ways we can try to stop such injustice.

7. Role Play

A. Getting Ready

In groups of 4 to 6 people discuss the following situation. Talk about what alternatives the store owner has. Also make notes about what the stranger, the store owner, and the family members would probably say.

You own a small business. One day a stranger walks in and tells you that you must pay him and his organization a certain sum every month as "insurance" against fire, accidents, and vandalism. You know from his threatening manner that he'll hurt you or your place of business if you don't agree to the monthly payments. After the stranger leaves, you discuss the problem with your family. Different people in the family have different ideas about what should be done.

B. Act It Out

Choose roles in your group—the stranger, the store owner, and the family members. Act out the two scenes of the role-play. During the family's discussion, try to reach a consensus about what to do.

20. Taking a Vacation

Have you ever tried to plan a vacation with someone whose interests were very different from yours?

1. Read and Evaluate

A: What do you want to do over spring vacation?

B: Why don't we go camping, since we could use some fresh air and peace and quiet.

coast
people think it is

A: Camping? That doesn't sound very interesting. I thought we might take a trip along the eastern **shoreline** and stay at motels. It's **supposed to be** beautiful in the spring.

B: That would be pretty expensive, wouldn't it? The motel would probably cost us at least $65 a night.

spend money for something special

A: I know, but vacations are a good time to **splurge** a little. We could travel comfortably, see different places, and meet new people.

bored

makes

escaping daily life

B: I get **tired of** talking to people every day, and driving from place to place **drives** me crazy. Aren't you interested in exploring nature and getting some exercise or just **getting away from it all**?

A: Well, we can explore the towns that we visit. That way, we won't have to sleep on the ground and freeze to death. Besides, seeing new places and learning about other people is a good experience. You can learn more about life that way than you can by going to the woods or the mountains.

have the same way of thinking

B: I guess we're just not on the **same wavelength**. Looks like we're on our own. Anyway, have a good time and don't get run over by any cars.

A: Yeah, you too. Good luck with the weather.

In class

2. Retell

Students may volunteer to describe the kind of person **A** is and the sort of choices that grow out of his/her personality. Do the same for **B**.

3. Analysis of Content

Work with a partner. Confirm the factors listed below for **A**. Mark the number of each one in the margin of the dialog at the place where it is confirmed. Each of you may make a similar list for **B**. Then your partner may identify the sentence in the dialog that confirms each point you have made. Can you think of any others?

A	B
1. trip along the shoreline	1.
2. meet people	2.
3. explore towns	3.
4. stay in comfortable places	4.
5. learn about different people	5.

4. Analysis of Discussion Techniques: Raising an Objection, Stating a Reason

Work as a class with your teacher to understand these discussion techniques. *Raising an objection* can be stated in a direct or an indirect way. *Stating a reason* may require the use of common connectors, such as *because of* and *since*, and may be stated directly or indirectly. Consider how tone of voice affects such techniques.

Raising an Objection

Examples: Don't you think that *might* be a little dangerous? (indirect)
I *cannot accept* sleeping on wet ground. (direct)
I *object to* spending my vacation in the city. (direct)
I'm thinking about my past experiences. (indirect)

What examples of raising objections can you find in the dialog?

Stating a Reason

Examples: The camping trip was cancelled *due to* the storm. (direct)
The older man was hired *because of* his work experience. (direct)
Rising prices for motel rooms *might have something to do with* his decision. (indirect)
It will be said we lost the game *since* our star player was sick (indirect)

What examples of stating reasons can you find in the dialog?

5. Practice

Work with a partner.

1. Look for an example of raising an objection in the dialog. Your partner may make a counterpoint. (Try to think of one that isn't used in the dialog.) Then you may do the same.
2. Follow the same procedure to find examples of stating reasons.

6. Discuss

Work in small groups. Discuss the following:

1. If both **A** and **B** asked you to go with them on vacation, whom would you rather *not* go with? Give reasons for your decision, using phrases such as *because, since, it might be, I'm worried about,* and so on.
2. When you take a vacation, what do you hope to get out of it? Rest? Adventure? New friends? List the things that are most important to you, in order of preference. Compare and discuss your choices with the other members of your group.

7. Role Play

A. Getting Ready

With a partner or in small groups, work out a plan for a trip together. Think about the details—place, means of travel, places to stay, day-time/nighttime activities, etc.—as you would like them to be.

B. Act It Out

Make the final plans, compromising in order to come to agreement. One of you may be the reporter and take notes. The reporter will describe the plans to the rest of the class.

21. Whom Should We Hire?

If you were hiring a new employee and had to choose between two qualified people, would you prefer experience to recent education? Age to youth?

Before class

1. Read and Evaluate

A: I'm not really sure which man we should hire. The older man has a lot of experience, but we need some young people in the company for the future.

B: There's no question in my mind that the older man would be better for these reasons. He's married and has three kids; he really needs the job; and we wouldn't have to train him.

A: Yes, but he's already 45, which means that he can probably only work for ten or fifteen years at the most, and working in the factory isn't an easy job for an older man. We'd also have to pay him more than the young guy.

B: Yes, but the young guy doesn't have any experience. And his high school grades weren't that good. I wonder if he could really do the job. We need someone we can depend on and who can accept responsibility.

strong desire

making friends

A: I don't think that training him would be a problem. Let's look at the positive points. He's **eager** to work; he's young, healthy and strong; and he'll be able to work for the company for a long time. And he shouldn't have any trouble **getting along with** the other employees. Sometimes older people have their own way of thinking.

good point

B: I think that is an **asset** if you want a leader. He has good recommendations and experience in directing people. We need some more leaders, too.

duty

A: If we put this person in a leadership position right away, that might create some problems among the other employees. But to get back to the young guy, I think we have a **social obligation** to hire some young people who don't have any work experience. How else can they get on-the-job training? He said that he would do anything.

considering the future

save money

B: Well, maybe **in the long run** you're right. I guess everyone deserves some kind of chance. But if we want some immediate results, we'd **be money ahead** with the older man.

In class

2. Retell

Describe the conversation about hiring a new employee. One student may call on others to supply details.

3. Analysis of Content

Work with a partner. Look at the factors (points) listed below for the older man. Find sentences in the dialog that confirm each factor. Mark the number of the factor next to the sentence in the dialog. Note that the factors are not listed in order. Then work together to complete the chart for the younger man.

Older Man	Younger Man
Advantages	**Advantages**
1. experience	
2. married, children	
3. no need to train	
4. good recommendations	
5. has directed men	
6. really needs job	
7. immediate results	
Disadvantages	**Disadvantages**
1. inflexible?	
2. cost more	
3. strength?	
4. work 10–15 years	
5. accepted by other men?	

4. Analysis of Discussion Techniques: Expressing Certainty, Introducing Supporting Evidence or Examples, Bringing the Discussion Back to Your Point Or the Main Point

Work as a class with your teacher to understand these discussion techniques. These three techniques often use introductory phrases.

Expressing Certainty

Examples: *I feel quite certain . . .*
There's no doubt in my mind . . .
I am convinced he will do a good job.

What examples of expressing certainty can you find in the dialog?

Introducing Supporting Evidence or Examples

Examples: *Consider these points.*
There are a number of factors to consider.
Let me present some examples. For one thing/first of all, . . .

What are some examples in the dialog?

Bringing the Discussion Back to Your Point or the Main Point

Examples: *Let's look at the question of . . . again.*
Let's not lose sight of the purpose of the discussion.
I think the point we were discussing was . . .
The original purpose of this discussion was . . .

What are some examples in the dialog?

5. Practice

Work with a partner. Look at the factors listed in the chart in Exercise 3. Consider each one from the point of view of an older woman candidate for the job. Consider the factors from the point of view of a younger woman. Are the counterpoints different, in your view?

6. Generalize

Work in small groups. Prepare lists, as directed below, and then discuss your list with your group members. Consider the matter of equal opportunity for men and women.

You have been appointed as the new personnel manager of your medium-sized company (150–200 employees). Before you can hire people, you have to determine the criteria by which you will judge the people. Make a list of the factors (criteria) you think are important and *rank-order* them (put the most important factor first and then the next important, etc.). Try to think of about ten factors. *Do this by yourself.* In small groups discuss your lists with each other.

7. Role Play

A. Getting Ready

Work in small groups. Decide on a position in a company for which you are going to conduct a personnel interview. Half of the group may plan what the personnel manager would say. You should ask questions about education, family situation, past work experience, health, reason for wanting the job, why the person thinks he/she is qualified for the job, etc. How would you ask these questions? The other half of the group will discuss the kinds of questions important to a job candidate: the nature of the work required, the reporting structure of the company, hours of work, training, health benefits, opportunity for advancement, salary, etc. How would you ask these questions?

B. Act It Out

Break into pairs. Each pair act out the job interview.

22. Save the Whales

If a culture depends on the killing of a creature for its survival and that creature is becoming scarce, which should be preserved—the culture or the creature?

Before class

1. Read and Evaluate

on the verge of dying off as a species

A: I just don't understand how anyone could kill and eat a whale. It's so cruel, especially when we know they are **on the brink of extinction**.

B: I don't think anyone really knows how many whales there are, since no international agency has actually counted them.

A: Does it really matter what the exact number is? No one has to kill them for food or protein, as some people argue. There are other sources of protein, such as beef.

B: That's easy for you to say, since you come from a beef-eating culture, but what about people whose local culture and livelihoods are based on the whale? Should they be denied their way of life? And what about people who don't have enough land or **feed** to raise cattle?

animal food

A: Why can't they import meat? Lots of countries have more meat than they can eat.

money, dollars

B: Well, you're right about the last point. But lots of countries don't have the **foreign exchange** to buy meat; and furthermore, even if they did, they wouldn't want to change their lifestyle or become dependent on other countries for their food.

natural life-chain system

destroyed

A: That may be true, but we mustn't overlook the fact that the whale is an important part of the overall **ecological system**. We have to protect them if we don't want them to be **wiped out** completely. Most people in the world agree. Why should a few people be so **arrogant** about satisfying their eating habits?

demanding

about 2.7 kg

B: That's an interesting question. Maybe some people would ask the same question of people who eat beef. After all, for every **six pounds** of grain that a cow eats, only one pound of meat is produced. When you consider that the major food in the world is **grain**, that's **pretty** wasteful, don't you think?

wheat, oats, corn, barley, etc.

rather

create and sell in very large numbers

A: But there's no comparison between killing a cow and killing a whale. We don't **mass-produce** whales. And furthermore, whales have brains, just as human beings. They can think. It's like killing a six-year-old child.

support

B: I doubt whether there is any scientific **evidence** to back up that last statement. But, anyway, the point I am trying to make is that how people live depends on their culture. We can't say what is absolutely right or wrong. People who hunt whales certainly don't

gone, disappeared from earth
to prevent

want to see them become **extinct**; but at the same time, they don't want to see their culture destroyed because of a total **ban** on whaling. We have to consider this problem from more than one point of view.

In class

2. Retell

One student may briefly summarize **A**'s argument. Another may summarize **B**'s position on the subject of saving whales.

3. Analysis of Content

Work with a partner. Find the sentence in the dialog that confirms each factor listed for **A** below. Put the number of the factor in the margin next to that sentence in the dialog. List the factors from **B**'s responses. Number the factors next to **B**'s lines in the dialog.

A	B
1. almost extinct 2. other sources of protein 3. can import meat 4. important part of ecological system 5. mass-produce beef, not whales 6. only to satisfy eating habits is arrogant 7. no comparison between killing whale and cow 8. whales similar to human beings	

4. Analysis of Discussion Techniques: Questioning an Action, Discounting or Minimizing the Other Person's Point, Challenging Indirectly

Work as a class with your teacher to understand these discussion techniques.

Questioning an Action

Examples: *I wonder why* anyone would want to do that?
Do you really believe that is the best course of action?
I don't see why you would want to do that.

What examples of questioning an action can you find in the dialog?

Discounting or Minimizing the Other's Point of View

Examples: *I don't think we have to worry about such things.*
I think most everyone can see that/knows that.
I guess it's only natural.
That's nothing new.

What examples of this discussion technique can you find in the dialog?

Challenging Indirectly

Examples: *Could you possibly cite some examples?*
I wonder if everyone will feel the same way.
There may be some question as to the validity of that statement.
There seem to be some other opinions, according to the reports I have read.

What examples of challenging indirectly can you find in the dialog?

5. Practice

Work with a partner. Look at **A**'s points, replacing the topic of saving whales with that of saving the elephant, which is being destroyed for its ivory. Or choose another creature. One of you will read **A**'s lines, substituting the new subject and changing reasons, as appropriate. The other will work through **B**'s lines in the same way. Do the discussion techniques work in the same way with your new topic?

6. Discuss

Work in small groups. Discuss whose point of view you think is more reasonable, **A**'s or **B**'s. Why? Use the discussion techniques practiced in this unit. Be persuasive, but not angry. Can your group reach a compromise?

7. Role Play

A. Getting Ready

Prepare to role-play a panel of leaders of an environmental group who are appearing on a TV program to debate the leaders of a fishermen's cooperative that is dependent on hunting whales for its livelihood. Half of the class may help the students who are to role-play the environmental group members. The other half of the class may help the students who are to represent the fishermen's cooperative. The fishermen's cooperative consists of independent men who work small boats, as compared with the huge industrial ships, which are high-profit ventures.

B. Act It Out

One student will be the moderator of this debate. This person's role is to introduce the program and the panel members, to give each side equal time to present its arguments, and to remind panel members, if necessary, to remain calm and reasonable. Perform the role play.

23. A One-Eyed Monster?

Commercial television is sometimes criticized for its portrayal of violence, sex, and materialism. Some people consider it a "one-eyed monster" because they feel that it influences viewers in a bad way. What is television like in your country? Does the government control programming? Do you feel that television has a good influence on viewers?

Before class

1. Read and Evaluate

expressing their opinions

improve

A: I'm glad to see that some people are **speaking out** about TV programming. With all the other things that the government controls for our health and welfare, you'd think they'd have the sense to **clean up** TV.

B: Clean up TV? What about freedom of speech?

A: That's the first thing that everyone says. But what about the bad influence of all that violence and sex on children? Why don't more people think about that? There have been cases in which children acted out the same crime or violent act that they had seen on TV.

exceptions

a cause-and-effect relationship

B: Except for those few **isolated cases**, though, is there any real evidence that TV is a bad influence? Some studies show a **positive correlation** and some don't. I don't think that anyone can say for sure. If anything, some kids no doubt see more violence in real life than on TV.

you can't really mean that

garbage; programs with nothing of value, just violence and sex

throw away

connection

society; everything that's going on beyond the walls of their homes

A: Oh, **come on**. Kids who watch TV regularly see thousands of killings and fights a year. It seems to me that there's such a thing as common sense. Who could possibly benefit from watching such **trash** day after day? Actually, when you consider all the programs on TV, there are very few worth watching. A person might as well **get rid of** his TV set.

B: Don't be ridiculous! Television is a major medium of communication in the world today. What about people who are handicapped or elderly? For them TV is a **link** to the **outside world** and a form of inexpensive entertainment. And certainly educational TV is valuable.

drastically changed

A: I wouldn't disagree with any of that, but we have to consider the effect of TV programs—the good and the bad—on the whole population. Think how many people waste their time staring at a TV set rather than reading a book or doing things with their families. Our lives have been **revolutionized** by TV.

B: Okay, TV may not be perfect. But to get rid of it would be impossible. Consider the economic effects. Think of all the people who make, sell, and service TV's. And the production, advertising, and broadcasting people. They'd all lose their jobs. .

A: I never said we should get rid of TV. What I am saying, though, is that if we want to live in a better society, the quality of TV programming should be improved.

In class

2. Retell

Students may summarize the substance of each argument about television.

3. Analysis of Content

Work with a partner. Look at the following list of arguments taken from this discussion. Decide whether each argument has social, economic or political/legal significance. Explain why you classified the arguments as you did.

1. To clean up TV would require some kind of controls. _____
2. Watching violence and sex may have a bad influence on children. _____
3. Television is a worldwide means of communication. _____
4. Television is an inexpensive form of entertainment. _____
5. Regulation of TV would be a violation of freedom of speech. _____
6. Handicapped and elderly people would probably be lonelier and bored without TV. _____
7. If people got rid of TV's, makers and sellers would lose their jobs. _____
8. Many people watch TV instead of doing more worthwhile things with family and friends. _____

9. If the number of programs were reduced, there would be less need for advertisements. _____

10. Better programming might improve society. _____

11. Watching TV has reduced the time spent reading. _____

12. A reduction in programs would result in a reduction of TV production and broadcasting staff. _____

4. Analysis of Discussion Techniques: Challenging Directly or Bluntly, Stating Opinions, Stating Facts

Work as a class with your teacher to understand these discussion techniques.

Challenging Directly or Bluntly

Examples: *Sick again*? What's the matter this time? (repetition of part of the other person's statement followed by a question)

You can't be serious./How can you say such a thing?/You must be joking.

Do you have any facts to back that up?

Don't you think that's a bit unrealistic/unfair/exaggerated/careless?

Stating Opinions

Examples: I think/feel/believe (that) . . .

In my opinion . . .

It seems to me (that) . . ./*If you ask me* . . .

There's no doubt in my mind (that) . . .

What examples of stating opinions do you find in the dialog?

Stating Facts

There are no particular words or phases that signal the beginning of a factual statement. Even if a person begins a statement with, "The facts are . . ." this does not necessarily mean that the content of the statement is fact.

What examples of evidence *claimed to be* fact do you find in the dialog?

5. Practice

Work with a partner. Read the statements in Exercise 2. Identify the discussion technique used in each sentence. You may choose to identify it as a form other than the three studied in this unit. Then go back and try to state it *another* way, making it a challenge, an opinion, or a fact. Your partner will tell you how he/she interprets your restatement. Is that what you meant your sentence to say?

6. Discussion

Work in small groups. Try to use the discussion techniques that you have learned. Are you for or against the regulation of TV programming? If you support regulation, to what extent, how, and by whom do you think it should be regulated?

7. Role Play

A. Getting Ready

Work in small groups. Discuss the reasons for having rules for TV-watching in a family. Consider a family that includes young *and* older children versus a family with teenagers only. Decide which family your group will role-play. What should the rules be?

B. Act It Out

One person will be the parent and one will be a thirteen-year-old. How can the parent persuade the young teenager to compromise his/her wishes about TV programs for the good of everyone in the family? Role-play just for your group. If there is time, others may do the role play. Change the sex of the parent and the child.

24. Please Don't Pick the Flowers

In your country, are people allowed to pick flowers that grow on public property?

Before class

1. Read and Evaluate

A: Do you ever go hiking in the mountains?

B: As often as I can. I like to look at the wild flowers.

A: Do you ever pick any of the flowers or bring them back with you and plant them in your garden?

Of course not!

B: Heavens no! I'd never think of it. Why do you ask?

A: Well, I was really surprised to see so many signs in the mountains saying not to pick the flowers. What harm can it do if I pick a couple on top of some isolated mountain?

B: I suppose lots of people ask the same question. But why should we destroy nature for our own pleasure? Flowers belong to everyone, not just to one person. If many people picked them, there might not be any left for other people to see.

A: That's hard to believe. There are millions of flowers in the mountains.

B: Yeah, but many of them are very rare and only grow in the mountains. That's why lots of people love to go to the mountains.

A: But in most cases the land is owned by the government so it's public land. I'm a taxpayer, so why can't I pick a flower or two? They aren't all rare.

B: I don't think it is a case of the land's being public or some flowers' being common and others rare. It's really a case of whether we want to preserve nature or let people destroy it by carrying it away.

simple thing to do

A: Do you really think that picking a flower is destroying nature? It's such an **innocent** act. Should children be denied such a simple pleasure? Or a lover the chance to show his love in such a natural way?

place

B: No, but the beauty of nature can only be truly enjoyed in its natural **setting**. If you want to pick some flowers, pick the ones in your garden; or if you want to give a flower to your lover, buy one. That way everyone can enjoy flowers.

a person with an absolute idea

A: You're a real **purist**, aren't you?

B: I'm concerned about our children's being able to enjoy the same things we can now. Your "isolated mountain" is no different from

114

results   a public park. If people don't consider the **consequences** of even the smallest act of destruction, then we might discover someday that there isn't any nature left to enjoy.

In class

2. Retell

Is there someone in the class who agrees, after this initial reading of the dialog, with **A**'s point of view? Someone who agrees with **B**? It might be interesting for them to summarize each side in the argument—with some spirit! If not, students may volunteer to summarize the substance of each side.

3. Analysis of Content

Work with a partner. Look at the points listed under **A** in the box below. Find the sentences confirming them in the dialog. Mark the number of the factor (point) in the margin of the dialog next to the sentence that confirms it. What are the factors in **B**'s responses? Complete the chart for **B**, and mark the confirming sentences in the dialog with each number.

A	B
1. picking a few flowers in isolated places doesn't hurt anything 2. unlimited number of flowers in mountains 3. public land belongs to everyone 4. picking one flower will not lead to destruction of nature 5. many ordinary flowers 6. picking flowers common natural pleasure of life	

4. Analysis of Discussion Techniques: Expressing Disbelief, Stating an Alternative Idea, Refocusing and Clarifying the Purpose of the Discussion

Work as a class with your teacher to understand these discussion techniques.

Expressing Disbelief

Examples: *Do you really believe that?*
You must be kidding!
Where did you get that idea?
Do you expect me to believe that?

What examples of expressing disbelief can you find in the dialog?

Stating an Alternative Idea

Stating an alternative idea is a way to present another solution to a problem or a way to reach a compromise.

Examples: *If you insist, then why not consider . . .*
One alternative might be/would be . . .
If we were to . . . , then everyone could benefit.

What examples of stating an alternative idea can you find in the dialog?

Refocusing and Clarifying the Purpose of the Discussion

Examples: *I think there has been some misunderstanding. What we are dealing with here is . . .*
I don't think this is a situation of . . . It's more a case of . . .

What example(s) of this technique can you find in the dialog?

5. Practice

Work with a partner. Use the examples in Exercise 4 to restate the arguments in the dialog. One of you may read **A**'s lines, and the other may read **B**'s lines. Use the expressions in Exercise 4 (or similar ones) as you present each point.

6. Discussion

Work in small groups. Discuss the following:

1. To what extent do you feel that people have the right to pick flowers, dig up, collect plants that grow in state/national forests or parks?
2. Many countries have undeveloped mountain or forest areas designated as "wilderness areas" or "nature preserves." Conservationists say that such areas should be left undeveloped to preserve the natural balance of the ecosystem. Others say that without road or other facilities, people can't enjoy such areas, and the beauty of nature is wasted. What is your view?

7. Role Play

A. Getting Ready

You will role-play a situation in which the government wants to build a modern highway through the mountains and beautiful natural areas so that more people can enjoy them. Divide the class in half. Select one person from one group to be a person representing the government. A person from the other group will represent the conservationists. Help the person selected from your group for the role play to develop his/her argument.

B. Act It Out

The two people will act out the role play for the class. Each must be very persuasive. Remember to be calm and reasonable, but present your case with conviction.

25. Increasing Military Spending

Do you think that spending money on weapons decreases or increases the likelihood of a country's being involved in a war?

Before class

1. Read and Evaluate

A: I read that the government is increasing military spending again. I can't understand why they think we need more weapons.

B: Every country has to protect its own interests. If you show weakness, some neighboring country may be **tempted** to bother you. Also, one never knows when an unfriendly government may come to power.

encouraged

A: I don't think our country has to worry about such things. If anything, our having weapons just makes our neighbors nervous. There is also the **temptation** for the military to play with their **new toys**. How do you control that problem? It's not just a question of outside **threat** but also the possibility of your own military gaining too much power and controlling the country.

desire
weapons
danger

B: Well, it's ridiculous to think that a nation can exist in this world without any kind of military. Even neutral countries like Sweden and Switzerland have a strong military. It's because of their capacity to defend themselves that no one bothers them.

A: I wonder. Maybe the fact that the world recognizes them as being neutral is the reason that no one bothers them. If we had a peace constitution and stated our neutrality to the world, world opinion would protect us.

B: Do you really believe that? You know, you can never tell when a country may want something that another country has, such as water or some important natural resource, like oil. I admit that most people would like to live in peace and not have to worry about war, but man by nature is not a peaceful animal. Furthermore, economic distress, social upheaval, and political crises can all lead to war. How do we **guard against** the unpredictable?

protect ourselves
from

A: You have to recognize the fact that some governments promote the manufacture of arms as a way to stimulate their domestic economies. I wonder if all countries really need arms or are they being **convinced** to buy them? What I'm trying to say is that countries that export weapons may create false feelings of fear and danger in order to increase their sales. Unfortunately, fear is a strong force in the world.

persuaded

119

B: Yes, and as long as it exists, we have to make sure that we can protect ourselves against it. The best defense is a good offense. I also would like to see military spending cut so that we could improve education and the quality of life, but I'm afraid that disarming would invite disaster.

A: And to continue to spread arms all over the world will also invite disaster. Your way can't create peace. It would only make a tense **standoff** based on a **balance of terror**. But my way does contain at least the hope of a real peace, and it reduces the chances that the entire world would be destroyed. Are you willing to live under constant threat of total destruction?

impasse

high levels of fear, caused by high levels of arms

In class

2. Retell

One student may summarize **A**'s arguments. Another may summarize **B**'s points.

3. Analysis of Content

Work with a partner. One of you may list the factors in **A**'s arguments, and the other may list **B**'s factors. Then exchange your lists, and find the sentences in the dialog that confirm each factor. Mark the number in the margin of the dialog. Check each other's work.

A
1.
2.
3.
4.
5.
6.

B
1.
2.
3.
4.
5.
6.

4. Analysis of Discussion Techniques: Reporting Information, Expressing Doubt, Using the Speaker's Previous Point to Strengthen Your Argument

Work as a class with your teacher to understand these discussion techniques.

Reporting Information (facts, opinions, rumors)

Examples: *According to the papers/his opinion . . .*
It has been reported that . . .
I understand that . . .
I have been told that . . .

What examples of reporting information can you find in the dialog?

Expressing Doubt

Examples: *I just can't see . . .*
There are some doubts in my mind as to whether that is best.
I really wonder if he knows what he is doing.
I'm not sure/certain/convinced that he can be trusted.

What examples of expressing doubt can you find in the dialog?

Using the Speaker's Previous Point to Strengthen Your Argument

There are many words and phrases that are ambiguous (have more than one meaning). We often take a word or phrase that another person has said and use it for our own benefit by changing the meaning. What examples of this discussion technique can you find in the dialog?

5. Practice

Work with a partner. Look again at the list of discussion techniques at the beginning of Part 3 (page 89). Find examples of these other techniques in the dialog in this unit. Make notations in the margin of the dialog to identify them.

6. Discussion

Work in small groups. Discuss the following questions. Use the discussion techniques you have learned in this unit, and others that you were reminded of in Exercise 5.

1. If your country were suffering from high unemployment but at the same time had the industrial capacity to manufacture weapons, tanks, planes, etc., would you be *for* or *against* manufacturing and selling arms as a way to reduce unemployment and improve the economy?
2. Do you think peace can best be achieved by:
   a. Balance of terror—meaning that both sides' military power is about the same and enough to destroy the world
   b. one or more countries' unilaterally disarming
   c. some other way

7. Role Play

A. Getting Ready

Divide the class in half. The first group may consider and role-play Situation 1, below. The second half may consider and role-play Situation 2. Discuss the points to be made on both sides of the question to help prepare the two people selected for each role play.

1. Increasing the military expenditure by 10 percent would mean cutting welfare expenditures by 6 percent. One person takes the role of a welfare representative who is opposed to the cut. Another person takes the role of a defense representative.

2. Education expenditures are going to be cut by 7 percent in order to increase defense expenditure. One person takes the role of an educator. Another person takes the role of a politician in favor of more defense spending.

B. Act It Out

The persons selected to role-play Situation 1 may perform it for the class. The persons who will role-play Situation 2 will role-play, again for the whole class.

26. *Is Government Welfare Necessary?*

Should the task of helping needy people be undertaken by the government or by private institutions and individuals?

Before class

1. Read and Evaluate

A: I wonder if the government knows how much money it is wasting on welfare?

B: What do you mean by wasting?

A: Well, when you consider the amount of money needed to operate the welfare offices, it seems like such a waste. The question I would ask is, why does the government have to be in the welfare business?

help

B: Who do you think is going to **take care of** handicapped people or the children of families where the father loses his job or the parents are killed in an accident?

A: There are a lot of religious organizations that help such people, and relatives of the family can help them. Some local communities also help their own people.

B: Yes, but there are too many cases where no one helps. And what happens when a person doesn't have any relatives to help or when the relatives live too far away?

A: I know there are some problems, but when the government begins to give away money, it just encourages some people to try to get something for nothing. That discourages other people's efforts to help people in need, since they know they are being taxed more by the government.

desire to help other
people

treated unfairly,
unequally

B: You may be right, but I think you are too optimistic about people's **sense of charity**. Sometimes people are **discriminated against** because they are handicapped. They want to live just like everyone else, but they don't want to beg for their survival. If they receive some money from the government, that gives them some degree of independence.

desire

wasted, thrown away

A: Okay, but there has got to be a better way to solve the problem. People pay high taxes to support the welfare system, but high taxes destroy the **incentive** to work harder. How can a country's economy grow if people know that their taxes are **going down the drain**? On top of such heavy taxes, why, they ask, should they give additional time and money to charity? In the end, no one feels

124

personally responsible anymore for the welfare of family, neighbors or community.

B: I doubt whether *all* the money is being wasted, and furthermore, not everything is measured in terms of economic growth. If you have any **sense of humanity**, you have to think of the **less fortunate** in the world and be willing to make some kind of sacrifice.

A: I agree, but I don't think that government welfare increases anyone's sense of humanity.

respect for mankind

people who have problems

2. Retell

Your teacher may select students to summarize the various points made by **A** and **B**.

3. Analysis of Content

Work with a partner. Identify the sentences in the dialog that confirm the factors listed below for **A**. Notice that they are not in the order of the dialog. Write the number of each in the margin next to the dialog. Write the factors for **B**. Identify them in the same way in the dialog.

A	**B**
1. administrative costs high	
2. private organizations and individuals help needy people	
3. relatives can help	
4. high taxes discourage contributions to charitable organizations—people feel they've already paid	
5. high taxes affect attitude toward work	
6. welfare burden on economy	
7. gov't. welfare doesn't make us more humanitarian	

4. Analysis of Discussion Techniques: Focusing the Discussion on a Specific Point, Pointing Out the Weakness of the Other Person's Argument, Overgeneralizing

Work as a class with your teacher to understand these discussion techniques.

Focusing the Discussion on a Specific Point

Examples: *What we should look at is . . .*
Let's consider this particular point.
Let's take a look at . . .
What we should ask is . . .

What are some examples in the dialog?

Pointing Out the Weakness of the Other Person's Argument

Examples: *The problem with that argument is that . . .*
I think you are overlooking some very important points. What about . . .
And what/how . . . when/if . . . ? Yes, but . . .

What are some examples in the dialog?

Overgeneralizing

Overgeneralizing is based on narrow opinions or false assumptions, frequently an exaggerated statement using words like: *never, always, no one, all, everywhere/one, only,* etc.

Examples: *Everyone* you meet in that city is either Italian or Irish.
That group at the university is *always* trying to cause trouble.
All the government cares about is taking our money.

What are some examples in the dialog?

5. Practice

Work with a partner. Look again at the list of discussion techniques at the beginning of Part 3 (page 89). Find examples of these other techniques in the dialog in this unit. Make notations in the margin of the dialog to identify them.

6. Discussion

1. Work as a class for the first part of this discussion. One student may make notes on the chalkboard as other students suggest all the kinds of welfare benefits they can think of. Another student can lead the class discussion of these questions:
   a. Are there some benefits that should be left in the hands of private people?
   b. Are there others you would like to add that are not now receiving government aid?
2. Work in small groups to discuss the following:

   Most people agree that society needs a "safety net" to save people who are in danger of starvation and other life-threatening crises. People disagree about how extended the net should be. Look over the statements below and tell which you agree and disagree with, explaining why and giving examples. Be persuasive as you express your personal values.

   It is the responsibility of the government to ensure that:

   ☐ no one starves to death or is malnourished.
   ☐ everyone has equal access to the best medical and dental care.
   ☐ elderly people are not poor and lonely.
   ☐ everyone has a job or an adequate income.
   ☐ everyone has adequate housing at a reasonable price.
   ☐ children receive a high-quality education for as many years as they desire.

7. Role Play

A. Getting Ready

Work in small groups to prepare to role-play a situation with a concerned citizen who would like to see some benefit provided or improved. The other person is a government official who listens and responds to the citizen's appeal. Choose from the many kinds of welfare benefits, including old-age benefits, unemployment insurance, medical services, day-care centers, and low rent housing. What techniques can you suggest to the persons who will do this role play? Think of the techniques and then work out examples for use in the role play.

B. Act It Out

Two persons may perform the role play for the small group. One or two of the performances may be given for the entire class.